THERE REALLY IS A DIFFERENCE!

A Comparison of Covenant
and Dispensational Theology

THERE REALLY IS A DIFFERENCE!

A Comparison of Covenant
and Dispensational Theology

RENALD E. SHOWERS

The Friends of Israel Gospel Ministry, Inc.
P. O. Box 908, Bellmawr, NJ 08099

THERE REALLY IS
A DIFFERENCE!

A Comparison of Covenant
and Dispensational Theology

Renald E. Showers

Copyright © 1990 by The Friends of Israel Gospel Ministry, Inc., Bellmawr, NJ 08099

Tenth Printing **2006**

Library of Congress Catalog Card Number: 90-80121
ISBN 0-915540-50-9

Visit our Web site at *www.foi.org*

DEDICATION

This book is dedicated to the people of First Baptist Church, DuBois, Pennsylvania, whose teaching, example, encouragement, and prayer support have contributed so much to my life and ministry over the years.

TABLE OF CONTENTS

FOREWARD

The study of theology is considered a dreary affair by all too many contemporary Christians. It is alarming to hear people say that they do not pay attention to doctrine but seek only to be involved, loving, practical Christians. One shudders to think what this philosophy will produce in the future. *We* practice what we believe to be true, so doctrine does make a difference! It reveals the very meaning of our existence and, therefore, provides the means to experience fulfilled and fruitful lives.

The Bible offers a systematic interpretation of history. It covers the entire scope of history from beginning to end, including the *what* and *why* of the future. It presents a unifying principle that ties together and makes sense of the whole gamut of events, distinctions, and successions. Consequently, it is imperative for every Christian to have a grasp of how to interpret or rightly divide the Word of God.

Currently two theological persuasions dominate efforts to systematically interpret Scripture. In this book Dr. Renald Showers draws the distinctions between Covenant and Dispensational Theology and demonstrates that the differences are not superficial but fundamental— *there really is a difference!*

Dr. Showers provides a valuable resource for those of us who are not theologians by writing clear, readable language and demonstrates the practical necessity of knowing what you believe. This volume will bring clarity, understanding, and perspective to your Bible study. The result can be a renewed sense of purpose, joy, and enthusiasm in your walk with God.

Elwood McQuaid
Editor-in-Chief
THE FRIENDS OF ISRAEL
GOSPEL MINISTRY, INC.

THERE REALLY IS A DIFFERENCE!

A Comparison of Covenant
and Dispensational Theology

ONE

WHAT IS IT ALL ABOUT?

The Restless Quest For Meaning

W hen man rebelled against God, he doomed himself to a restless, unending search for meaning to life and history. Throughout most of his existence on planet Earth, man has been plagued by three major questions: Where have we come from? Why are we here? Where are we going? This compulsion for meaning has driven scientists to probe space and philosophers to build systems of thought. It has prompted Pilate and countless others to ask, "What is truth?" (Jn. 18:38). It is an underlying factor in what has been called *the midlife crisis*. It has even motivated Hollywood to produce a satirical motion picture entitled "The Meaning Of Life."

Philosophy Of History

Throughout time, man has made numerous attempts to deal with the issue of meaning in a systematic, organized fashion. The result of each attempt could be called a philosophy of history. What is a philosophy of history? Karl Lowith defines it as "a systematic interpretation of universal history in accordance with a principle by which historical events and successions are unified and directed toward ultimate meaning."[1]

According to this definition, a philosophy of history has certain characteristics. First, it offers a systematic interpretation of history. In other words, it explains the *why* of historic events in an organized way. Second, it covers the whole scope of history from beginning to end. It explains why things happened in the past, why the world is where it is in the present, and the *what* and *why* of the future. Third, a philosophy of history has a unifying principle which ties together and makes sense of events, distinctions, and successions. Fourth, it assigns ultimate meaning to history. It demonstrates that the flow of history has an ultimate goal or purpose, that events are not disjointed or unrelated to each other, and that future events are the grand climax toward which all previous events have been moving.

The Bible deals with the issue of meaning. It offers a systematic interpretation of history. It covers the entire scope of history from beginning to end, including the *what* and *why* of the future. It presents a unifying principle which ties together and makes sense of the whole gamut of events, distinctions, and successions. The Bible demonstrates that history has an ultimate goal or purpose. Because the Bible does these things, it can be said that the Scriptures present a philosophy of history. However, since the Bible is God's written revelation to man, it is God's philosophy of history. This means that it presents the ultimate, authoritative philosophy of history.

The Necessary Elements Of A Valid Exposition Of The Biblical Philosophy Of History

Over the course of years, Bible scholars have attempted to develop different expositions of the biblical philosophy of history.[2] For an exposition to be valid, it must contain certain necessary elements. First, *it must contain an ultimate purpose or goal for history toward the fulfillment of which all history moves.*

Second, *it must recognize distinctions or things that differ in history*. The biblical record of history indicates that distinctions or things that differ have existed during the course of history. At first glance, some of these appear to be contradictory. For example, *Jesus gave two distinct gospels to His disciples to preach*. The content of the first gospel was, "The kingdom of heaven is at hand" (Mt. 10:7; cf. 9:35; Mk. 1:14-15).

Paul defined the second gospel in 1 Corinthians 15:1-5 when he said: "Moreover, brethren, I declare unto you the gospel which I preached unto you,...By which also ye are saved,...that Christ died for our sins...And that he was buried, and that he rose again the third day...and that he was seen."

An examination of these gospels indicates that their contents were quite distinct. This was made even more obvious by Matthew. After the disciples had been out for some time preaching the first gospel, they returned to Christ to report on their ministry. Matthew records, "From that time forth began Jesus to show unto his disciples, how he must go unto Jerusalem, and suffer many things from the elders and chief priests and scribes, and be killed, and be raised again the third day" (Mt. 16:21). The language indicates that although the disciples had already been preaching one gospel, up to this point Jesus had never told them about His coming death, burial, and resurrection. Therefore, the first gospel contained nothing concerning Jesus' death, burial, and resurrection. Peter's negative reaction to Jesus' new teaching emphasized the distinction in the gospels very strongly: "Then Peter took him, and began to rebuke him, saying, Be it far from thee, Lord; this shall not be unto thee" (Mt. 16:22). If Peter had already been preaching Jesus' death, burial, and resurrection, he would not have reacted so negatively when Christ referred to these coming events.

In addition, *Christ gave two distinct commissions to His disciples.* When He gave them the first gospel, He commissioned them to go to "the lost sheep of the house of Israel" but not to the Gentiles and Samaritans (Mt. 10:5-6). Later, in conjunction with the second gospel, He commissioned them to preach to all creatures (Mk. 16:15) and to make disciples of all nations (Mt. 28:18-20).

Jesus also commanded distinct preparations for the ministries of the disciples. When He commissioned them to preach the first gospel just to Israel, He ordered the disciples not to take money, a bag, two tunics, sandals, or a staff (Mt. 10:9-10). However, when it became obvious that Israel would reject Jesus and His first gospel, and when the second gospel was about to become a reality, Jesus commanded the disciples to take a purse, a bag, and even a sword (Lk. 22:35-36).

The Bible presents *distinctive ways of God's dealing with people guilty of adultery.* While the Mosaic Law was in effect, God commanded the Jews to put such people to death (Lev. 20:10). Since the death of Christ, God does not command this (1 Cor. 6:9-11).

God has also had *distinctive ways of dealing with murderers.* Prior to the Noahic flood, God did not command the death penalty for murderers (Gen. 4:1-15), but after the flood, He has ordered it (Gen. 9:5-6; Rom. 13:1-7).

Throughout history, God has employed *different dietary laws.* Prior to the flood, God permitted only a vegetarian diet (Gen. 1:29). After the flood, He permitted man to eat the flesh of all forms of animal life (Gen. 9:3). While the Mosaic Law was in effect, God forbade the Jews to eat the flesh of certain kinds of animals (Lev. 11).

These and all other biblical distinctions must not be ignored, watered down, or explained away if an exposition of the biblical philosophy of history is to be valid.

A third necessary element of a valid exposition of the biblical philosophy of history is that *it must have a proper concept of the progress of revelation.* The Bible indicates that God's truth has been revealed in stages at different points in history. God did not give all of His revealed truth to man in one lump sum at the beginning of history. For example, God did not reveal the fact that there would be a Redeemer until after the fall of man (Gen. 3:15). God did not reveal the practice of capital punishment until after the flood (Gen. 9:5-6). While Jesus was here in His first coming, He did not reveal everything that He wanted His disciples to know (Jn. 16:12). He indicated that the Spirit of God would reveal the additional truth to them after Christ's ascension (Jn. 14:26; 16:13). Paul talked about truth which had been hidden from people in past ages of history but was revealed to him and others in New Testament times (1 Cor. 2:6-10; Eph. 3:2-6). In light of this progress of revelation, in order for an exposition of the biblical philosophy of history to be valid, it dare not read the content of later revelation back into earlier revelation. It must not make the earlier revelation say all that the later revelation said.

The fourth necessary element is that *it must have a unifying principle which ties the distinctions and progressive stages of revelation together and directs them toward the fulfillment of the purpose of history.* A valid exposition of the biblical philosophy of history must be able to tie the distinctions and stages of revelation together into one, unified whole in a sensible way. It also must demonstrate how these things contribute to the fulfillment of history's goal.

Fifth, *it must give a valid explanation of why things have happened the way they have, why things are the way they are today, and where things are going in the future.* An exposition of the biblical philosophy of history must be able to explain how, when, and why such things as murder, false religions, capital punishment, human government, different languages, different nations, anti-Semitism, the Church, Roman Catholicism, Islam, the Renaissance, and the Reformation began. Why did the Holocaust of World War II happen? Why is there a modern state of Israel in existence? Why is the present Middle East crisis taking place?

Sixth, *it must offer appropriate answers to man's three basic questions*: Where have we come from? Why are we here? Where are we going?

Two Basic Approaches To The Biblical Philosophy Of History

Within the last three to four hundred years, Bible-believing scholars have developed two distinct approaches to expositing the Bible's philosophy of history. Each approach has produced a system of theology. Those two systems are known as Covenant Theology and Dispensationalism. The next several chapters will examine both systems.

TWO

AN EXAMINATION OF COVENANT THEOLOGY

A Simple Definition Of Covenant Theology

C ovenant Theology can be defined very simply as a system of theology which attempts to develop the Bible's philosophy of history on the basis of two or three covenants. It represents the whole of Scripture and history as being covered by two or three covenants.

The History Of Covenant Theology

Covenant Theology did not begin as a system until the 16th and 17th centuries. It did not exist in the early Church. Louis Berkhof, a prominent Covenant Theologian, wrote, "In the early Church Fathers the covenant idea is not found at all."[1] Nor was the system developed during the Middle Ages or by the prominent Reformers Luther, Calvin, Zwingli, or Melanchthon.

According to Berkhof, Kaspar Olevianus (1536-1587) was the real founder of a well-developed Covenant Theology "in which the concept of the covenant became for the first time the constitutive and determinative principle of the whole system."[2] The system started in the Reformed Churches of Switzerland and Germany and passed to the Netherlands, Scotland, and England. In 1647 the Westminster

Confession of Faith in England became the first confession of faith to refer to Covenant Theology.[3]

In the Netherlands, Johannes Cocceius played a significant role in making Covenant Theology widely accepted through his publication in 1648. In Cocceius' treatment, "the whole development of sacred history is governed by this thought" (the covenant idea).[4] A later writer, Herman Witsius (1636-1708), tied the covenant idea together with the eternal decrees of God.[5] This gave rise to the idea that in eternity past God determined to govern the whole course of history on the basis of one or two covenants.

Covenant Theology was introduced to America primarily through the Puritans. Major examples of prominent Covenant Theologians of the 19th and 20th centuries are Charles Hodge of America and Herman Bavinck and Abraham Kuyper of Holland.

A Description Of Covenant Theology

As noted earlier, Covenant Theology attempts to develop the Bible's philosophy of history on the basis of covenants. Covenant Theologians disagree concerning the number of these covenants. Some say there are two (the Covenant of Works and the Covenant of Grace). Others say there are three (the Covenant of Redemption, the Covenant of Works, and the Covenant of Grace). Those who propose only two covenants combine the Covenant of Redemption and the Covenant of Grace. For example, Shedd writes,

> Though this distinction (between the covenant of redemption and the covenant of grace) is favored by Scripture statements, it does not follow that there are two separate and independent covenants....The covenant of grace and redemption are two modes or phases of the one evangelical covenant of mercy.[6]

Berkhof claims that most Covenant Theologians favor the three-covenant view. In light of this, this study will examine that view.

The Covenant Of Redemption

According to Berkhof, the Covenant of Redemption was established between God the Father and God the Son. In this covenant the Father granted the Son to be Head and Redeemer of the elect. In return, the Son voluntarily agreed to take the place of those whom the Father had given Him.

The Covenant of Redemption was established in eternity past. God knew that man would fall away from Him; thus, in eternity past God determined to provide redemption during the course of history for the elect.[7]

The Covenant of Redemption placed certain requirements upon the Son:

> The Father required of the Son...that He should make amends for the sin of Adam and of those whom the Father had given Him, and should do what Adam failed to do by keeping the law and thus securing eternal life for all His spiritual progeny.[8]

This involved the Son's becoming human, yet without sin, and being placed under the Mosaic Law.

In return for what the Son would do in providing redemption, the Father promised several things to the Son: resurrection (Ps. 16:8-11; Acts 2:25-28), a numerous seed (Ps. 22:27; 72:17), all power in Heaven and earth (Mt. 28:18; Eph. 1:20-22; Heb. 2:5-9), and great glory (Jn. 17:5; Phil. 2:9-11).[9]

According to Berkhof, there is a threefold relationship between the Covenant of Redemption and the Covenant of Grace. First, the Covenant of Redemption is the eternal model after which the historical Covenant of Grace is patterned. Second, the Covenant of Redemption is the foundation of the Covenant of Grace. It makes the Covenant of Grace possible. Third, the Covenant of Redemption provides the means for the establishment and execution of the Covenant of Grace.[10]

The Covenant Of Works

According to Covenant Theology, the Covenant of Works was established between the triune God and Adam. In this covenant God made Adam the representative head of the human race, so that Adam could act for all his descendants.

The Covenant of Works was established between the creation and fall of man. Thus, unlike the Covenant of Redemption, it was made during the course of world history.[11]

In the Covenant of Works God required "implicit and perfect obedience" of Adam.[12] Adam was placed on probation temporarily in order to determine whether he would willingly subject his will to the will of God.

God promised eternal life (not natural life) to Adam and his descendants in return for Adam's perfect obedience. Berkhof admits that no such promise is stated in the Bible, but "the threatened penalty clearly implies such a promise."[13]

Since Adam was appointed representative head of the human race, if he were to disobey God, he and his descendants would be penalized with death, "including physical, spiritual, and eternal death."[14]

The Covenant Of Grace

According to Covenant Theology, God established the Covenant of Grace because Adam broke the Covenant of Works. Berkhof defines the Covenant of Grace as "that gracious agreement between the offended God and the offending but elect sinner, in which God promises salvation through faith in Christ, and the sinner accepts this believingly, promising a life of faith and obedience."[15] This definition clearly indicates that the first party of the Covenant of Grace is God, who acts as a gracious, forgiving Father.

Covenant Theologians disagree concerning the second party of the covenant. Berkhof says, "It is not easy to determine precisely who the second party is."[16] Some say the second party is the sinner; others say it is the elect or the elect sinner in Christ; still others say it is believers and their seed.[17] Berkhof is convinced that the Covenant of Grace "is fully realized only in the elect," but "the covenant as a historical phenomenon is perpetuated in successive generations and includes many in whom the covenant life is never realized."[18] In other words, even some people who never become regenerate are included in the Covenant of Grace.

How can the Covenant of Grace include both those who become regenerate and some who never become regenerate? According to Berkhof, the Covenant of Grace has two aspects. It exists both as "a communion of life" and as "a purely legal relationship."[19] Only the regenerate experience the covenant as a communion of life, for only they enter fully into the spiritual life intended by the covenant. But both the regenerate and their children experience the covenant as a legal relationship. This means, then, that unregenerate children of believers are in the Covenant of Grace. They enter the covenant by virtue of their physical birth to parents who are in the covenant.[20]

What is involved in experiencing the Covenant of Grace as a legal relationship? To express it another way, how are the unregenerate children of believers in that covenant? Berkhof gives a fourfold answer to these questions. First, "They are in the covenant as far as their responsibility is concerned."[21] They are responsible to repent and believe.

Second, "They are in the covenant in the sense that they may lay claim to the promises which God gave when He established His covenant with believers and their seed."[22] God promised to produce spiritual life in the seed of believers. This does not mean that God will save every child of every believer, for His promise was "given to the seed of believers collectively, and not individually."[23] But it does mean that children of believers exist in a privileged position, for "as a rule God gathers the number of His elect out of those who stand in this covenant relationship."[24]

Third,

> They are in the covenant in the sense that they are subject to the ministrations of the covenant. They are constantly admonished and exhorted to live according to the requirements of the covenant. The church treats them as covenant children, offers them the seals of the covenant, and exhorts them to a proper use of these. They are the guests who are first called to the supper, the children of the kingdom, to whom the word must be preached first of all, Matthew 8:12; Luke 14:16-24; Acts 13:46.[25]

Fourth, "They are also in the covenant as far as the common covenant blessings are concerned."[26] Unregenerate children of believers are subject to certain special ministries of the Holy Spirit. The Spirit strives with them, convicts of sin, enlightens in a measure, and gives blessings of common grace (Gen. 6:3; Mt. 13:18-22; Heb. 6:4-6).[27]

When these children reach their years of discernment, they are responsible to accept their covenant obligations voluntarily by entering the communion of life aspect of the covenant through a true confession of faith.[28] But what happens to a person who does not do this? "If one who stands in the legal covenant relationship does not enter upon the covenant life, he is nevertheless regarded as a member of the covenant."[29]

Berkhof made one other interesting observation concerning such children: "As long as the children of the covenant do not reveal the contrary, we shall have to proceed on the assumption that they are in possession of the covenant life."[30]

The Establishment, Requirements, Promise

Covenant Theologians disagree concerning when in history the Covenant of Grace was established. Some believe that it was established immediately after Adam's fall, when God gave the first promise of the Redeemer (Gen. 3:15). Others take a different view. Berkhof states that Genesis 3:15 was the first revelation of the Covenant of Grace, but it was not the formal establishment of that covenant.[31] The covenant was not established until God's covenant with Abraham (Gen. 12). "The establishment of the covenant with Abraham marked the beginning of an institutional Church." Before Abraham "there was what may be called 'the church in the house'...families in which the true religion found expression..., but there was no definitely marked body of believers, separated from the world, that might be called the Church."[32] Thus, Berkhof sees the Church in the Old Testament and appears to equate the beginning of the Church with the establishment of the Covenant of Grace.

Although Berkhof is convinced that the Covenant of Grace was not formally established until Abraham's time, he also is convinced that believers before Abraham were in the Covenant of Grace. "The Abrahamic Covenant did not include the believers that preceded him and who were yet in the covenant of grace."[33]

Covenant Theology claims that the Covenant of Grace requires several things of those people who are in it. It requires faithful, devoted love, agreement to be God's people, saving faith in Christ, continual trust in Christ forever, and a life of obedience and consecration to God.[34]

The main promise which God made in the Covenant of Grace is "I will...be a God unto thee, and to thy seed after thee" (Gen. 17:7). However, this main promise includes the following promises: temporal blessings, justification, adoption, eternal life, the Spirit of God with His many ministries, and final glorification.[35]

On the basis of biblical statements to the effect that Jesus is the Mediator of the New Covenant (Heb. 8:6; 9:15; 12:24), Covenant Theologians have concluded that Christ is the Mediator of the Covenant of Grace.[36]

The Relationship Of The Covenant Of Grace To The Dispensations And The Progress of Revelation

Covenant Theologians recognize that there have been different dispensations and progress of revelation through the course of world history. For example, in the Netherlands, Johannes Cocceius (1603-1669) recognized three dispensations after the fall of man. He called the first *ante legem* (before the Law), the second *sub lege* (under the Law), and the third *post legem* (after the Law).[37]

Traditionally, however, most Covenant Theologians have preferred to divide postfall history into two major dispensations. Berkhof said,

> It is preferable to follow the traditional lines by distinguishing just two dispensations or administrations, namely, that of the Old, and that of the New Testament; and to subdivide the former into several periods or stages in the revelation of the covenant of grace.[38]

Ernest Frederick Kevan, principal of London Bible College, London, England, expressed it this way:

God's covenanted purpose with sinful man has ever been one of grace; but the covenant of grace was based on a double plan, or, to use scriptural terminology, was revealed in two dispensations. The first of these was the Mosaic dispensation sometimes called the "Old Covenant," and the second is the Christian dispensation, usually called the "New Covenant."[39]

Covenant Theologians claim that the Covenant of Grace exists throughout these dispensations. In spite of some differences in administration between the dispensations, it is the same Covenant of Grace which is being administered. Kevan declared that in the strictly biblical sense the word *dispensation* "is used in the Scriptures to make only one distinction, that is, the distinction between the way the grace of God was made known before the coming of Christ and the way it was manifested after his redeeming work had been accomplished...strictly, the covenant is one and the same covenant of grace all through,"[40] To Kevan's way of thinking, then, it is rather improper to speak of Old Covenant and New Covenant.[41]

Berkhof said that the Covenant of Grace:

is essentially the same in all dispensations, though its form of administration changes.[42]

· ·

Now it is undoubtedly true that there is considerable difference between the administration of the covenant before and after the giving of the law, but the similarity is greater than the difference.[43]

· ·

The covenant of Sinai was *essentially* the same as that established with Abraham, though the form differed somewhat.[44]

• •

> The covenant of grace, as it is revealed in the New Testament, is essentially the same as that which governed the relation of Old Testament believers to God.[45]

According to Covenant Theology, each dispensation or covenant named in the Bible is simply another stage of the progressive revelation of the nature of the Covenant of Grace throughout history. George N. M. Collins, minister of Free St. Columba's Church, Edinburgh, Scotland, wrote,

> Throughout the OT period there were successive proclamations of this covenant. We find it in the *protevangelium* of Gen. 3:15. Certain of its provisions were later revealed to Noah (Gen. 9). It was then established with Abraham (Gen. 12), and with his descendants after him, thus becoming a national covenant. Although in the NT this covenant is described as *new*, such passages as Romans 4 and Galatians 3 show that it is essentially one with the covenant under which believers lived in OT times....But although the same covenant, it is described as a *better* covenant under the NT dispensation, because it is now administered not by Moses, a servant, but by Christ the Son (Heb. 3:5,6).[46]

Covenant Theologians present several proofs for the existence of the Covenant of Grace throughout the dispensations. First,

> The summary expression of the covenant is the same throughout, both in the Old and New Testament: "I will be thy God." It is the expression of the essential content of the covenant with Abraham, Gen. 12:7, of the Sinaitic covenant, Ex. 19:5; 20:1, of the covenant of the plains of Moab,

Deut. 29:13, of the Davidic covenant, 2 Sam. 7:14, and of the new covenant, Jer. 31:33; Heb. 8:10.[47]

Second, "The Bible teaches that there is but a single gospel by which men can be saved. And because the gospel is nothing but the revelation of the covenant of grace, it follows that there is also but one covenant."[48]

Third, "The Mediator of the covenant is the same yesterday, today, and forever (Heb. 13:8)."[49] The point of this proof is that if the Mediator (Christ) is the same throughout history, the covenant which He mediates must also be the same throughout history.

Fourth,

> The way of salvation revealed in the covenant is the same. Scripture insists on the identical conditions all along, Gen. 15:6, compared with Rom. 4:11; Heb. 2:4; Acts 15:11; Gal. 3:6-7; Heb. 11:9. The promises, for the realization of which the believers hoped, were also the same, Gen. 15:6; Ps. 51:12; Matt. 13:17; John 8:56. And the sacraments, though different in form, have essentially the same signification in both dispensations, Rom. 4:11; 1 Cor. 5:7; Col. 2:11,12.[50]

Here Berkhof used the term *sacraments* to refer to circumcision and baptism.

Key Elements
Of Covenant Theology's Exposition
Of The Biblical Philosophy Of History

Earlier it was noted that in order for an exposition of the biblical philosophy of history to be valid, it must contain certain necessary elements. Now that Covenant Theology has been surveyed as a system, it is essential to determine how it deals with those necessary elements as it attempts to exposit the Bible's philosophy of history.

As was seen earlier, the first necessary element of a valid exposition is an ultimate purpose or goal for history toward the fulfillment of which all history moves. Because Covenant Theology emphasizes the Covenant of Grace as God's means of working His purpose throughout history, and because it defines that covenant as "that gracious agreement between the offended God and the offending but elect sinner, in which God promises salvation through faith in Christ, and the sinner accepts this believingly, promising a life of faith and obedience,"[51] it would appear that Covenant Theology sees the ultimate goal of history as being the glory of God through the redemption of the elect.

The second necessary element is the recognition of distinctions or things that differ in history. Covenant Theology states that distinctions after the fall of man are different administrations of the same Covenant of Grace.

The third necessary element is a proper concept of the progress of revelation. As it deals with this concept, Covenant Theology sees each new body of truth which is revealed as simply another stage of the progressive uncovering of the nature of the Covenant of Grace.

The fourth necessary element is a unifying principle which ties the distinctions and progressive stages of revelation together and directs them toward the fulfillment of the purpose of history. Covenant Theology's unifying principle for history after the fall of man is the Covenant of Grace.

AN EVALUATION OF COVENANT THEOLOGY

Commendable Features Of Covenant Theology

I n its attempt to exposit the Bible's philosophy of history, Covenant Theology has several commendable features. First, its emphasis upon the grace of God, the redemptive work of Christ, and salvation by grace through faith has been most commendable. These are crucial areas of God's truth which must be emphasized, and Covenant Theologians have done some of the finest work of researching and expounding these great doctrines.

Second, Covenant Theology is to be commended for its recognition of Jesus Christ as the central figure of world history. This recognition is exactly on target, for Jesus Christ is truly the key to the accomplishment of God's purpose for history.

Third, Covenant Theology has made an honest attempt to be faithful to the Scriptures while expositing the biblical philosophy of history. This motivation to be faithful is precisely what it should be because God intends the Bible to be the authority for what man believes and practices.

Problem Features Of Covenant Theology

Space will not permit a thorough evaluation of Covenant Theology; therefore, only some of the problems involved with this system of thought can be examined at this point.

First, Covenant Theology's ultimate goal of history is too limited or narrow. As noted in the previous chapter, Covenant Theology sees the ultimate goal of history as being the glory of God through the redemption of the elect. Although the redemption of elect human beings is a very important part of God's purpose for history, it is only one part of that purpose. During the course of history, God not only has a program for the elect but also a program for the nonelect (Rom. 9:10-23). In addition, God has different programs for nations (Job 12:23; Isa. 14:24-27; Jer. 10:7; Dan. 2:36-45), rulers (Isa. 44:28-45:7; Dan. 4:17), Satan (Jn. 12:31; Rom. 16:20; Rev. 12:7-10; 20:1-3), and nature (Mt. 19:28; Acts 3:19-21; Rom. 8:19-22). Since God has many different programs which He is operating during the course of history, all of them must be contributing something to His ultimate purpose for history. Thus, the ultimate goal of history has to be large enough to incorporate all of God's programs, not just one of them.

Second, Covenant Theology denies or weakens some of the distinctions which are in the Bible by insisting that distinctions are simply different phases of the same Covenant of Grace. For example, Covenant Theology nullifies the genuine distinction between the Abrahamic Covenant and the Mosaic Covenant (the Law). Berkhof wrote, "The covenant of Sinai was *essentially* the same as that established with Abraham, though the form differed somewhat."[1] But, if these two covenants were essentially the same, why did Paul emphasize their distinctiveness in Galatians 3? For example, in Galatians 3:18 Paul asserted that if the inheritance is based on the Law of the Mosaic Covenant, it cannot at the same time be based upon the promise of the Abrahamic Covenant.

In addition, Covenant Theology denies the existence of distinctive gospels in the Bible. By contrast, it was demonstrated in the first chapter that there are indeed different gospels in the Bible.

Covenant Theology insists that there is no essential distinction between the Mosaic Covenant (the Law) and the New Covenant. Berkhof declared that when Paul, in 2 Corinthians 3, contrasted the ministry of the Law with the ministry of the New Covenant, he had in mind the ministry of the Law as it was perverted by Jews long after the Law was given, not the ministry of the Law as it was given by God.[2] But the language of 2 Corinthians 3:3-11 will not permit this approach. It indicates that the Law about which Paul talked is the Law which was engraved on stones, not a Jewish perversion of that Law.

In 2 Corinthians 3 Paul emphasized the fact that the Mosaic Covenant and the New Covenant are not essentially the same. The Law of the Mosaic Covenant was written on tablets of stone (external) [v. 3], but the Law of the New Covenant is written on tablets of human hearts (internal) [v. 3]. The Mosaic Covenant Law was a ministry of death (vv. 6-7), but the New Covenant is a ministry of life (v. 6). The Mosaic Covenant Law is a ministry of condemnation (v. 9), but the New Covenant is a ministry of righteousness (v. 9).

The language of Jeremiah 31:31-34 also indicates that the Mosaic and New Covenants are not essentially the same. In verse 32 God declared that the New Covenant would not be like the Mosaic Covenant. Anderson said that here God "speaks of a new covenant, not a covenant renewal, and thereby assumes a radical break with the Mosaic tradition."[3]

Covenant Theology also denies the distinction between the nation of Israel and the Church. As noted earlier, Covenant Theology believes that the Church existed in Old Testament times and that Israel was a major part of the Church in the Old Testament. It often defines the Church as the continuing covenanted community. In other words, the Church consists of all the peoples throughout history who have had a covenant relationship with God. Thus, these peoples are essentially the same. Because this issue of Israel and the Church being distinct is a major point of difference between Covenant and Dispensational Theology, it will be dealt with more in depth in a future chapter. For now, the following is asked: If it is true that the Church existed in the Old Testament and that Israel and the Church are the same, why did Jesus place the building of His Church in the future beyond the time that He spoke in Matthew 16:18, and why did the Apostle Peter call the Day of Pentecost (Acts 2) "the beginning" (Acts 11:15)?

Third, Covenant Theology is mistaken when it teaches that each of the biblical covenants is a continuation and newer phase of the Covenant of Grace. This mistake becomes apparent, for example, when it deals with the New Covenant. As noted earlier, Covenant Theologians equate the New Covenant with the Covenant of Grace which they claim has been in existence since the fall of man or Abraham. They claim that the New Covenant in the New Testament is essentially the same as the Covenant of Grace in the Old Testament. Covenant Theologians assert that the word *new* does not permit the conclusion that there is an essential contrast between the New Covenant in the New Testament and what existed in the Old Testament.

It is important to note that the words which are translated *new* in the Book of Hebrews will not permit these assertions of Covenant Theology. The word which is translated *new* for the New Covenant in Hebrews 12:24 refers to "what was not there before," "what has only just arisen or appeared," and what is "new in time or origin."[4] In other words, the New Covenant is something brand new. It was not in existence before Christ died. This would not be true if the New Covenant were simply a continuation of a covenant which has been in existence since early Old Testament history.

The word which is translated *new* for the New Covenant in Hebrews 8:8, 13, and 9:15 refers to "what is new and distinctive as compared with other things," "what is new in nature, different from the usual,"[5] and what is "new in kind."[6] Thus, the New Covenant established at Christ's death is different in nature or kind from what went before. It "is essentially different from the old divine order."[7] This is the exact opposite of what Covenant Theology says.

The fact that Covenant Theology is mistaken when it teaches that each biblical covenant is a continuation and new phase of the Covenant of Grace becomes apparent again when it deals with the Mosaic Covenant (the Law). It asserts that the Mosaic Covenant was a newer phase of the Covenant of Grace which had been initiated hundreds of years before the Mosaic Covenant. But it is a fact that the Mosaic Covenant instituted required conditions which had not been introduced before. Thus, if the Mosaic Covenant were a newer phase of the Covenant of Grace, it would be adding new conditions to that long-established covenant. Such an addition would violate a principle which Paul taught in Galatians 3:15 when he declared that once a covenant has been ratified, no one adds conditions to it.

Fourth, Covenant Theology's unifying principle is too limited or narrow. The Covenant of Grace is the factor which Covenant Theology employs to unify history either from the fall of man or the time of Abraham. This unifying factor is too limited in at least two respects. First, the Covenant of Grace deals only with God's redemption of the elect. It does not unify the program of redemption with all of God's other programs. Second, since the Covenant of Grace did not begin until the fall of man at the earliest, it does not unify prefall history with postfall history, which the unifying principle of a valid exposition of the biblical philosophy of history must do.

Fifth, in order to make its system work, Covenant Theology must employ a double hermeneutic (a double system of interpretation). Covenant Theology recognizes that the historical-grammatical method of interpreting the Bible is normal. In this method, attention is focused upon historical background and grammar to determine the correct meaning of a passage. Words are given the common, ordinary meaning which they had in the culture and time in which the passage was written. Covenant Theology also recognizes that the employment of another method of interpretation could lead to disaster when seeking the meaning of a passage.

In spite of these recognitions, Covenant Theology uses a second method of interpretation when dealing with certain areas of biblical teaching. This is especially true in its treatment of prophetic teachings concerning the future, particularly the future of the nation of Israel and the future Kingdom of God. In these areas, Covenant Theology frequently employs the allegorical or spiritualizing method. In this method words are not given the common, ordinary meaning which they had in the culture and time in which the passage was written. Instead, they are assigned different meanings. For example, according to this method, the word *Israel* does not have to mean the nation of Israel. It could mean the Church. Thus, according to this method, the prophetic promises of future blessing for Israel do not have to be fulfilled with the nation of Israel. Rather, they are to be fulfilled with the Church.

One major problem with the allegorical method of interpreting unfulfilled prophetic Scriptures is that thus far the prophetic Scriptures which have been fulfilled have been fulfilled in accordance with the historical-grammatical method of interpretation, not in accordance with the allegorical method. This would seem to indicate the manner in which God intends prophetic passages to be interpreted. In light of this and the fact that Covenant Theology recognizes the danger of employing the allegorical method when interpreting other areas of biblical teaching, one could ask by what authority Covenant Theology uses the allegorical method when interpreting the prophetic Scriptures.

This chapter has called attention to several significant shortcomings of Covenant Theology as it attempts to exposit the biblical philosophy of history. Future chapters will examine the alternative approach to that biblical philosophy — namely, Dispensationalism.

AN INTRODUCTION TO DISPENSATIONAL THEOLOGY

A Simple Definition Of Dispensational Theology

D ispensational Theology can be defined very simply as a system of theology which attempts to develop the Bible's philosophy of history on the basis of the sovereign rule of God. It represents the whole of Scripture and history as being covered by several dispensations of God's rule.

The History Of Dispensational Theology

Dispensational Theology did not exist as a developed system of thought in the early Church, although early Church leaders did recognize some of the biblical principles which are basic to Dispensational Theology.[1] For example, Clement of Alexandria (150-220 A.D.) recognized four dispensations of God's rule.[2] Augustine (354-430 A.D.) noted the fact that God has employed several distinct ways of working in the world as He executes His plan for history. Augustine used the term *dispensation* when referring to these different ways.[3] It must be said, however, that these Church leaders did not develop these recognized principles into a system of thought. They were not Dispensational Theologians.

The first person on record to develop a genuine dispensational scheme in a systematic fashion was the French philosopher Pierre Poiret (1646-1719). In his work entitled *The*

Divine Economy: or An Universal System of the Works and Purposes of God Towards Men Demonstrated, Poiret developed a scheme of seven dispensations covering the scope of Scriptures and history. This work was published in Holland in 1687.[4]

In 1699 John Edwards (1639-1716) published a well-developed dispensational scheme in his book entitled *A Compleat History or Survey of All the Dispensations.*[5] Isaac Watts (1674-1748 A.D.), the famous hymn writer and theologian, presented a system of six dispensations in an essay named "The Harmony of all the Religions which God ever Prescribed to Men and all his Dispensations towards them."[6]

During the 19th century the Plymouth Brethren, including one of their key leaders, John Nelson Darby (1800-1882), played a very significant role in developing, systematizing, and spreading Dispensational Theology.

Dispensationalism has been developed and promoted even further during the 20th century through the *Scofield Reference Bible.* This work, which was published originally in 1909, was primarily the work of Congregationalist pastor and Bible teacher C. I. Scofield. Scofield had been taught the Scriptures and Dispensationalism initially by the famous Presbyterian pastor and Bible teacher, Dr. James H. Brookes.[7] He produced the reference notes for the Bible after years of personal Bible study and months of intensive work in the libraries of the leading universities of Europe.[8] The impact of the *Scofield Reference Bible* is indicated by two facts. It was the first publication of Oxford University Press of New York to attain a sale of one million copies.[9] In addition, in recognition of this work, Scofield was elected to membership in the Societe Academique d'Histoire Internationale, the most influential of European literary societies.[10]

The rise of Bible and prophecy conferences and the Bible school movement since the late 1800s has also been a great aid to the spread of Dispensational Theology. Most Bible colleges and institutes, such as Philadelphia College of Bible, have consistently been dispensational in their teaching. On the seminary level the same has been true of Dallas Theological Seminary.

A very significant treatment of Dispensational Theology in the latter half of the 20th century is the book entitled *Dispensationalism Today* by Charles C. Ryrie.

The Meaning Of The Word *Dispensation*

The word which is translated *dispensation* in the New Testament is *oikonomia*, from which the English word *economy* is derived. The New Testament word is a combination of two words — *oikos*, which means *house*, and *nemo*, which means *to dispense, manage, or hold sway*.[11] Thus, the word literally means *house dispensing* or *house managing*.

It "relates primarily to household administration."[12]

The English word *dispensation* sometimes refers to "the system by which things are administered" and "the divine administration or conduct of the world." Theologically it is "A religious order or system, conceived as divinely instituted, or as a stage in a progressive revelation, expressly adapted to the needs of a particular nation or period of time."[13]

The English word *economy* in its theological usage refers to "The method of the divine government of the world, or of a specific department or portion of that government."[14]

The Usage Of The Word For Dispensation In The New Testament

The word *oikonomia* appears nine times in the New Testament. In six of these appearances (Lk. 16:2-4; 1 Cor. 9:17; Eph. 3:2; Col. 1:25) it is translated *stewardship* or *dispensation* and refers to a responsible office or ministry entrusted to one's care by a higher authority. In the other three appearances (Eph. 1:10; 3:9; 1 Tim. 1:4) it is translated *dispensation, fellowship,* and *edifying* in the King James Version and *administration* in the New American Standard Bible. In these three passages it refers to a particular way of God's administering His rule over the world. Ephesians 1:10 is of special interest, for it appears to refer to the particular way that God will administer His rule in the coming Millennium (the Millennial Dispensation). Ephesians 3:9 and 1 Timothy 1:4 refer to the particular way that God administers His rule now (the present dispensation).

Definition Of The Term *Dispensation* As It Relates To Dispensational Theology

In light of the usage of the word for dispensation in· the New Testament, the term *dispensation* as it relates to Dispensational Theology could be defined as *a particular way of God's administering His rule over the world as He progressively works out His purpose for world history.*

Essential Characteristics Of Each Dispensation

In order for each dispensation to be distinct from all other dispensations, it must have three essential characteristics. First, it must have a particular way of God's administering His rule. Each dispensation is characterized by a unique ruling factor or combination of ruling factors. Second, it must involve a particular responsibility for man. Each dispensation makes man responsible to obey God in accordance with its unique ruling factor or combination of factors. Third, it must be characterized by divine revelation which had not been given before. In order for man to know God's new way of ruling and his new responsibility, he must have these things revealed to him. Each new dispensation requires new revelation from God.[15] For example, Paul indicated that the present dispensation is definitely related to new revelation which God gave to the apostles and New Testament prophets (Eph. 3:2-10).

Secondary Characteristics Of Each Dispensation

The fact that each new dispensation involves a newly revealed responsibility for man indicates that each dispensation also has three secondary characteristics. First, each dispensation applies a test to man. The nature of the test is whether or not man will perfectly obey God's rule by fulfilling the responsibility which is characteristic of that dispensation. Second, each dispensation demonstrates the failure of man to obey the particular rule of God which characterizes that dispensation. Third, each dispensation involves divine judgment because of man's failure.[16]

Some Important Considerations

In order to understand the approach of Dispensational Theology to the Bible's philosophy of history, several important points of clarification must be taken into consideration. First, the different dispensations are different ways of God's administering His rule over the world. They are not different ways of salvation. Throughout history God has employed several dispensations but only one way of salvation. Salvation has always been by the grace of God through faith in the Word of God, and God has based salvation on the work of Jesus Christ.

Second, a dispensation is not an age of history, even though a dispensation may cover the same time period as an age. A dispensation is a particular way of God's administering His rule, but an age is a particular period of time.

Third, a dispensation may involve a particular way of God's administering His rule over all of mankind or over only one segment of mankind. For example, the Dispensation of Human Government was over all of mankind, but the Dispensation of the Mosaic Law was over only the nation of Israel.

Fourth, a new dispensation may continue or discontinue some ruling factors of previous dispensations, but it will have at least one new ruling factor never introduced before. Dispensational Theologians normally name each new dispensation after the new ruling factor or factors.

Fifth, each new dispensation demands new revelation. God must reveal His new way of ruling and man's new responsibility near the beginning of each dispensation. Since Dispensational Theology recognizes several successive dispensations, it has a strong concept of progressive revelation.

Concluding Remarks

Numerous things in the Bible indicate that God has employed different dispensations or ways of administering His rule throughout history. For example, before the Noahic Flood God did not institute capital punishment for murderers (Gen. 4:9-15), but He did institute it after the flood (Gen. 9:5-6). Between the giving of the Mosaic Law and the death of Christ, God commanded that adulterers in Israel be put to death (Lev. 20:10; Dt. 22:22; Jn. 8:5), but since the death of Christ God does not so command (1 Cor. 6:9-11). While the Mosaic Law was in effect, God required Jews to worship on Saturday (Ex. 20:8-11), but since the death of Christ God does not so require (Rom. 14:4-9; Col. 2:13-17). God's people today do not offer animal sacrifices for sins, but people before Christ's death were required to do so.

FIVE

AN EXAMINATION OF
DISPENSATIONAL THEOLOGY

T he majority of Dispensational Theologians are convinced that the Scriptures reveal seven dispensations of God's rule which cover the scope of history. This chapter will examine those seven recognized dispensations.

The Dispensation Of Innocency

Traditionally Dispensational Theologians have called the first dispensation the Dispensation of Innocency. Since Dispensational Theologians normally name each new dispensation after its new ruling factor or factors, it might be better to call the first dispensation the Dispensation of an Unconfirmed Favorable Disposition. The reason for this suggested name will be seen later.

The first dispensation began with the creation of man and ended with the fall of man from God. The Scripture portion which covers this dispensation is Genesis 1:26-3:24.

The ruling factor which God used to govern man during the first dispensation was an unconfirmed favorable disposition. Before man fell, he was favorably disposed toward God. Adam and Eve fellowshipped with God. They obeyed God by cultivating the Garden of Eden in accordance with His will. They did not run and hide from Him when He approached them. These things indicate that man originally had a disposition which was favorably oriented toward God.

It should be noted, however, that this favorable disposition was unconfirmed. This means that man was not locked into it forever. He could lose it by his own choice.

Man's favorable disposition toward God was unconfirmed because man had not chosen it for himself. It had been given to him by God at the time of his creation. When God created Adam, He gave him this type of disposition in accordance with His own sovereign choice. He did not show Adam all the types of dispositions which were possible and then give him the option of deciding which type he wanted.

The only way that man's favorable disposition could become confirmed was for man to be confronted with an alternative to being favorably disposed toward God and then for him to choose to remain favorably disposed.

The special revelation which God gave to man for the first dispensation is recorded in Genesis 1:28-29; 2:15-17, 24. God revealed that man was to abstain from eating the forbidden fruit and was to cultivate and keep the Garden of Eden. As male and female, human beings were to live together in a marital, one-flesh relationship, reproduce themselves, and exercise dominion over animal and plant life.

Man's responsibility during the first dispensation was to obey God on the basis of his unconfirmed favorable disposition toward Him. This responsibility subjected man to the following test: Would man obey God on the basis of his unconfirmed favorable disposition?

Man failed the test. Satan entered the garden and confronted him with an alternative to being favorably disposed toward God. The alternative was for man to reject God's rule over him and assert his own self-rule — just as God is His own Self-Ruler. Man chose to adopt this alternative rather than to remain favorably disposed toward

God. He displayed his choice outwardly by eating the forbidden fruit in violation of God's command.

Man's failure resulted in judgment which consisted of several tragic consequences. Man died spiritually as soon as he made his fateful choice (Gen. 2:16-17). A great separation took place between man and God. Man lost his favorable disposition toward God and replaced it with a disposition of enmity against God (Rom. 8:7). This is evident from the fact that Adam and Eve hid from God when He entered the garden to talk with them after their original sin. Because man had chosen to go this route, this disposition of enmity was a confirmed disposition. Man was so thoroughly locked into it that he could not rescue himself from it. Only the redemptive work of God could accomplish such a rescue.

In addition to spiritual death, man became subject to disease, deformity, accidents, and physical death. The woman was cursed with pain in childbirth and with the desire to rule the man. The ground was cursed, thereby making man's work of growing food much more difficult. Man lost his perfect environment. Because man followed Satan's lead to rebel against God's rule, Satan was able to usurp the rule of the world system away from God temporarily. Instead of living in a world system ruled by the benevolent God who loved him, man was doomed to live in a world system dominated by a tyrant who would use man for his own selfish ends.

In the midst of this dismal tragedy, at the end of the first dispensation God gave a ray of hope. In Genesis 3:15 He pronounced the first promise of the Redeemer who would be born of woman into the world during the course of history. As God progressively worked out His purpose for history, two of the great things which He would accomplish through the Redeemer would be the provision of redemption for fallen man and the defeat of Satan.

The Dispensation of Conscience

The second dispensation extended from the fall of man through the Noahic Flood. The Scripture which covers this dispensation is Genesis 4:1-8:19.

Inasmuch as man had lost his favorable disposition toward God, that ruling factor of the first dispensation was no longer available. As a result, in the second dispensation God administered His rule over man in a different way. It appears that He used two ruling factors to govern man during the new dispensation. The first new ruling factor was the human conscience. In Romans 2:14-15 the Apostle Paul indicated that human beings have a conscience. That the conscience functions as a ruling factor over human beings is evident, for Paul declared that it caused pagan Gentiles to "do by nature the things contained in the law," even though they had never been given the Mosaic Law. Paul also indicated that the conscience is the awareness of good and evil which exists inside of human beings.

Genesis 3:5 and 22 indicate that man obtained this awareness of good and evil as a result of eating the forbidden fruit. In other words, the human conscience began when man rebelled against God. Since the conscience functions as a ruling factor over human beings, it became one of the ruling factors of the new dispensation. Because of this, Dispensational Theologians have chosen to name the second dispensation after this new ruling factor.

The second ruling factor which God began to use in the second dispensation was the restraint by the Holy Spirit. In Genesis 6:3 God talked about His Spirit striving with man during the days prior to the Noahic Flood. The verb which is translated *strive* signifies *to rule*.[1] Thus, the Holy Spirit was also a ruling factor during the second dispensation.

In Genesis 4:3-7 God accepted Abel's blood sacrifice but rejected Cain's bloodless sacrifice. This implies that the special revelation which God gave to man for the second dispensation was that man was to approach God only by means of a blood sacrifice (cf. Heb. 11:4). Sinful man, no matter how sincere, could not come to God in his own way. He could come only in the one way that God had ordained.

Man's responsibility during the second dispensation was to obey God on the basis of his conscience and the restraint by the Holy Spirit. This responsibility subjected man to the following test: Would man obey God on the basis of his conscience and the restraint by the Holy Spirit?

Man failed the test miserably. Cain refused to bring the kind of sacrifice which God required. When God rejected his improper sacrifice, Cain became so enraged that he murdered Abel. Cain then began to build a godless civilization which became characterized by polygamy and violence. By Noah's day "the wickedness of man was great in the earth" and "every imagination of the thoughts of his heart was only evil continually" (Gen. 6:5). Things had become so bad that God could find only one righteous man left — Noah.

This serious failure brought horrible judgment. Through a worldwide flood, God destroyed the perverted segment of mankind. Through the ark, God preserved Noah and his family. In essence, God wiped the slate clean in order to give man a fresh start.

It should be noted that murder began as the result of man's rebellion against God's rule and that the flood took place because of that rebellion and God's judgment of it.

The Dispensation Of Human Government

The third dispensation extended from the Noahic Flood to the call of Abraham. The Scripture portion which covers this dispensation is Genesis 8:20-11:32.

Inasmuch as man had failed to obey God on the basis of his conscience and the restraint by the Holy Spirit during the second dispensation, once the flood ended God started a new dispensation by instituting a new ruling factor. Since the fountainhead of all human corruption prior to the flood was the continued existence of the first murderer, Cain, God determined that never again would He allow murderers to infect the rest of humanity with their rebellious attitudes. Shortly after Noah and his family left the ark, God ordained capital punishment for murderers (Gen. 9:5-6).

Capital punishment necessitates a human government agency to administer the sentence of execution. God required that the murderer's blood be shed by man. Thus, when God ordained capital punishment, He was thereby instituting human government as a further restraint against the lawless rebellion of man. In Romans 13:1-7 the Apostle Paul indicated that governmental authority derives its existence from God, that it was ordained for the purpose of restraining evil, and that it functions as the minister of God when it uses the sword for capital punishment.

Human government, then, with its authority to administer capital punishment, was the new ruling factor which God instituted for the third dispensation. Human conscience and the restraint by the Holy Spirit continued on as ruling factors in this new dispensation (indeed, Rom. 2:14-15, 2 Th. 2:7, and other passages indicate that they continue as ruling factors even into today's dispensation). Thus, the third dispensation had three ruling factors which God used to govern man: human conscience, the restraint by the Spirit, *plus* human government. Dispensational Theologians have named the third dispensation after the new ruling factor, since that is the factor which made the third dispensation distinct from the second.

The special revelation which God gave to man for the third dispensation is recorded in Genesis 9:1-17. God commanded man to multiply and populate the earth. He indicated that animals would now have a fear of man. God made animals a source of food for man. He promised that there would be no more universal floods, and He required the execution of murderers.

Man's responsibility during the third dispensation was to obey God on the basis of human conscience, restraint by the Holy Spirit, and human government. This responsibility subjected man to the following test: Would man obey God on the basis of these three ruling factors?

Man also failed this test of the third dispensation. Noah became drunk, which led to an indiscretion on the part of his son, Ham. Through time Noah's descendants rebelled against God's command to populate the whole earth (Gen. 11:4). In order to prevent their scattering over the entire earth, they began to build the city and tower of Babel.

This failure brought God's judgment. Up to this time Noah's descendants spoke only one language (Gen. 11:1). This universal language enabled them to work together on their building project. God judged these rebels by confusing their language. For the first time man began to speak different languages. This brought the building project to a halt because the builders could no longer understand each other's speech. It also caused Noah's descendants to separate from each other and relocate to different areas of the earth. Thus, they would begin to populate the entire earth.

Through time this beginning of different languages caused the development of nations. Thus, different languages and nations began as the result of man's rebellion against God's rule and God's judgment of that rebellion.

The Dispensation Of Promise

The fourth dispensation extended from God's call of Abraham to the giving of the Mosaic Law at Mount Sinai. The Scripture portion which covers this dispensation is Genesis 12-Exodus 18.

Since man had failed to obey God on the basis of human conscience, the restraint by the Holy Spirit, and human government, God started a fourth dispensation by instituting promise as a new ruling factor. The fact that promise began as a significant factor with God's special dealings with Abraham is made evident by such passages as Galatians 3:15-22 and Hebrews 6:13-15. A principle is a ruling factor if it makes a difference in the way people live. God intended His promises to Abraham and his descendants to make a difference in the way that they would live. Hebrews 11:8-30 demonstrates the fact that God's promises did make such a difference in the lives of Abraham and his descendants. Thus, promise functioned as a ruling factor.

The fourth dispensation had four ruling factors which God used to govern Abraham and his descendants: human conscience, the restraint by the Holy Spirit, human government, *plus* divine promise. Dispensational Theologians have named the fourth dispensation after the new ruling factor, since that is the factor which made the fourth dispensation distinct from the third.

The special revelation which God gave to Abraham and his descendants for the fourth dispensation is recorded in Genesis 12:2-3; 13:14-17; 15, 17:1-22; and 22:16-18. God made personal promises to Abraham: He would bless him, make his name great, give him many physical descendants, make him the father of a multitude of nations, give him the land of Canaan for an everlasting possession, and bless those who blessed him and curse those who cursed him.

God made national promises concerning Israel: He would bring Israel into existence as a nation and make it great, give Israel the land of Canaan forever, and establish the Abrahamic Covenant with the nation as an everlasting covenant.

God also made a universal promise: He would give blessing to all families of the earth through Abraham's line of descent (the Redeemer would come through Israel).

The responsibility of Abraham and his descendants during the fourth dispensation was to obey God on the basis of human conscience, the restraint by the Holy Spirit, human government, and promise. This responsibility subjected Abraham and his descendants to the following test: Would they obey God on the basis of these four ruling factors?

Abraham and his descendants failed the test of the fourth dispensation. On several occasions they disobeyed God as the result of lapses of faith concerning the fulfillment of His promises. Abraham fathered Ishmael through Hagar. Twice he lied concerning his wife Sarah. Isaac lied concerning Rebekah. Jacob was a great deceiver. The Jews did not return from Egypt to Canaan after the famine of Joseph's time ended. Apparently they forgot that their destiny was related to the land of Canaan rather than to Egypt.

This failure brought divine judgment. Throughout their history the Jews have continued to have problems with Ishmael's descendants. Through time they were subjected to slavery and threatened with annihilation in Egypt.

The Dispensation Of The Mosaic Law

The fifth dispensation extended from the giving of the Mosaic Law at Mount Sinai to the death of Jesus Christ on the cross at Mount Calvary. The tearing of the veil in the Temple in Jerusalem when Christ died indicated that the Law was terminated at that time. The Scripture portion which covers this dispensation is Exodus 19:1 through Matthew 27:56, Mark 15:41, Luke 23:49, and John 20:30.

Since Abraham and his descendants had failed to obey God on the basis of the four ruling factors of the fourth dispensation, God began a fifth dispensation by instituting the Mosaic Law as a new ruling factor.

The fifth dispensation had five ruling factors which God used to govern the people of Israel: human conscience, the restraint by the Holy Spirit, human government, promise, *plus* the Mosaic Law. The central core of the Mosaic Law was written on tables of stone. The Law inflicted the death penalty upon those who broke a number of its precepts. Thus, the Mosaic Law was a totally external way of God's administering His rule over Israel. For this reason, the Apostle Paul declared that the Mosaic Law functioned as a pedagogue (an external moral restrainer, Gal. 3:23-25). Dispensational Theologians have named the fifth dispensation after the new ruling factor because that is the factor which made the fifth dispensation distinct from the fourth.

The special revelation which God gave to Israel for the fifth dispensation is recorded in Exodus 20-Deuteronomy. It consisted of the Mosaic Law with its 613 commandments. These gave in detail God's will for the moral, civil, and ceremonial aspects of Israel's life.

Israel's responsibility during the fifth dispensation was to obey God on the basis of human conscience, the restraint by the Holy Spirit, human government, promise, and the Mosaic Law. This responsibility subjected the Jews to the following test: Would they obey God on the basis of these five ruling factors?

The people of Israel failed the test of the fifth dispensation. The Jews broke the Mosaic Law repeatedly (Jer. 31:32; Ezek. 16). God was forced to tell them that they had a heart of stone (Ezek. 36:26; Zech. 7:12). This was His way of saying that their inner control center was inflexible. It refused to bend, to conform to the Mosaic Law as an expression of God's rule over them. Also, during this dispensation Israel rejected its Messiah and had Him crucified.

This failure brought God's judgment upon Israel. The nation suffered many judgments during the fifth dispensation. Among the worst were the Assyrian and Babylonian captivities and Israel's temporary removal from its place of blessing (Rom. 11) and worldwide dispersion as the result of its rejection of Christ.

The Dispensation Of Grace

Before the sixth dispensation is examined, several important truths concerning the grace of God should be considered. First, in the Scriptures the grace of God deals with far more than salvation from sin. For example, it was by the grace of God that Noah survived the flood (Gen. 6:8), that Israel was restored to its homeland after the Babylonian captivity (Ezra 9:8), and that the afflicted were sustained in their trials (Prov. 3:34). It is by the grace of God that believers are given spiritual gifts and ministries (Rom. 12:6; Gal. 2:9). Indeed, the grace of God has so many facets that Peter called it "the manifold grace of God" (1 Pet. 4:10).

Second, although the grace of God was functioning throughout Old Testament times, it began to function in some new sense as a result of the ministry of Jesus Christ in His first coming. John indicated this when he wrote, "the law was given by Moses, but grace and truth came by Jesus Christ" (Jn. 1:17). John appeared to be making this new function of grace parallel with the function of the Mosaic Law. The Mosaic Law never functioned as a way of salvation (Gal. 2:16), but it did function as a rule of life (a ruling factor). In light of this, John is saying that grace began to function as a rule of life (a ruling factor) as a result of Christ's ministry in His first coming.

Third, other passages indicate that grace began to function as a ruling factor as a result of Christ's ministry. Paul wrote to believers in the present (sixth) dispensation, "ye are not under the law but under grace" (Rom. 6:14). In this passage the function of grace which Paul had in mind is parallel with the function of the Mosaic Law. In other words, grace has now taken over the function which the Mosaic Law had in the previous dispensation. As noted earlier, the Mosaic Law never functioned as a way of salvation, but it did function as a ruling factor. Thus, the function of grace which Paul had in mind in this passage is that of a ruling factor. This is indicated further by the word *under* which implies being under rule.[2] Paul was saying that believers in the present dispensation are now under grace, rather than the Mosaic Law, as a ruling factor. Thus, while grace continues to function as the way of salvation during this present (sixth) dispensation, it has assumed the additional function of a ruling factor as a result of Christ's ministry in His first coming.

In Titus 2:11-12 Paul indicated that one of the functions of the grace of God is that of "Teaching us that, denying ungodliness and worldly lusts, we should live soberly, righteously, and godly, in this present world." The word *teaching* means to "practice discipline, correct, give guidance."[3] Thus, Paul was saying that grace practices discipline over believers for the purpose of prompting them to reject a godless lifestyle and to adopt a godly one. Paul stated that the grace of God is functioning as a ruling factor "in this present world." The word which is translated *world* means *age.*[4] Grace is the ruling factor which uniquely characterizes the dispensation during this present age.

The sixth dispensation extends from the death of Jesus Christ to His Second Coming. (The author is presenting the majority view concerning the time when the present dispensation will end. Although some Dispensationalists believe that the Tribulation period will involve a separate dispensation, the majority have held that the sixth dispensation will not terminate until the Second Coming. For a discussion of the relationship of the Tribulation period to the present dispensation, see Charles C. Ryrie, *Dispensationalism Today*, pp. 54-57.) The Scripture portion which covers this dispensation is Matthew 27:57; Mark 15:42; Luke 23:50; and John 19:31 through Revelation 19:21.

Israel clearly demonstrated man's inability to obey God on the basis of the five ruling factors (including the external Mosaic Law) of the fifth dispensation. Thus, God began a sixth dispensation by instituting His grace as a new ruling factor.

During most of its course, the sixth dispensation has five ruling factors which God uses to govern people: human conscience, the restraint by the Holy Spirit, human government, promise, *plus* grace. It should be noted that the Mosaic Law is not a ruling factor in the present dispensation. God intended it to be in effect only until the ministry of Christ (Gal. 3:19, 23-25; cp. Rom. 6:14; 1 Cor. 9:20). It also should be noted that the restraint by the Holy Spirit will be removed as a ruling factor when it is time for the Antichrist to be revealed near the end of this dispensation (2 Th. 2:7-8). As a ruling factor for the believer, grace consists of two things: a confirmed favorable disposition toward God (the law of God in the heart, Rom. 7:22; 2 Cor. 3:3-11; Heb. 8:8-12) and the indwelling Holy Spirit (1 Cor. 6:19-20). Dispensational Theologians have named the sixth dispensation after the new ruling factor because that is the factor which makes the sixth dispensation distinct from the fifth.

The special revelation which God gave for the sixth dispensation is recorded in the latter part of the Gospels, the Book of Acts, the Epistles, and Revelation 1-19. Unsaved Jews and Gentiles are to receive the gift of righteousness through faith in Christ. The organized Church is to fulfill the Great Commission, to maintain a pure membership, to discipline unruly members, to prevent false teaching from existing within it, and to contend earnestly for the true faith. Individual believers are to live sensible, godly lives, to be associated with a local church, to evangelize and make disciples, and to use spiritual gifts properly.

Man's responsibility during the sixth dispensation is to obey God on the basis of human conscience, the restraint by the Holy Spirit, human government, promise, and grace. This responsibility subjects man to the following test: Does man obey God on the basis of these five ruling factors?

Man fails the test of the sixth dispensation. The majority of unsaved Jews and Gentiles do not accept the gift of righteousness. Organized Christendom does not fulfill the Great Commission, maintain a pure membership, discipline unruly members, prevent false teaching from existing within it, and contend earnestly for the true faith. Individual believers do not always live sensible, godly lives, associate with a local church, evangelize and make disciples, and use spiritual gifts properly. By the end of this dispensation, the unsaved will stage a major revolt against God's rule (Ps. 2:1-3; Rev. 16:12-16; 19:17-21), and organized Christendom will be very apostate (Rev. 17).

This failure during this present dispensation brings God's judgment and chastisement. God chastens and even brings premature physical death to some believers for disobedience (Acts 5:1-6; 1 Cor. 5:1-5; 11:27-32; Heb. 12:5-13; 1 Jn. 5:16). He puts some local churches out of existence (Rev. 2:5). Toward the end of the dispensation God will remove the Holy Spirit's restraint of evil (2 Th. 2:7-8), apostate organized Christendom will be destroyed (Rev. 17:16), God will pour out divine judgments upon the world (Rev. 6-19), and God will crush the revolt of the unsaved (Rev. 19:17-21).

The Dispensation Of The Millennium

Traditionally, Dispensational Theologians have called the seventh dispensation the Dispensation of the Millennium. Since Dispensational Theologians normally name each new dispensation after its new ruling factor or factors, it might be better to call the last dispensation the Dispensation of the Righteous Reign of Christ. The reason for this suggested name will become obvious.

The seventh dispensation will begin after the Second Coming of Christ and will end immediately before the release of Satan from the abyss and his final revolt. The Scripture portion which covers this dispensation is Revelation 20:1-6.

Apparently the seventh dispensation will have three ruling factors which God will use to govern the world: human conscience, human government, *plus* the theocratic rule of Christ. Inasmuch as the seventh dispensation will be the final one, it will be characterized by the final fulfillment of the promises which God made to Abraham and his seed. Once promises are fulfilled, they cease to be promises. Thus, promise will no longer be a ruling factor in the last dispensation. In addition, although salvation will continue to be by grace throughout the seventh dispensation, grace will not function as a ruling factor. The evidence for this is that during the theocratic rule of Christ, those who rebel against that righteous rule will be executed (Isa. 11:3-4; 29:20-21), and those nations which refuse to go up to Jerusalem to worship the King and celebrate the Feast of Booths will be punished (Zech. 14:16-19).

The most significant ruling factor of the seventh dispensation will be the righteous rule of Christ over the entire earth (Isa. 11:1-5; Zech. 14:9; 10). The world will have a theocratic government in which the rule of God will be administered worldwide through His representative, Jesus Christ.

The special revelation which God gave concerning the seventh dispensation is contained in numerous Old Testament passages (passages dealing with some of the major biblical covenants and prophecies concerning characteristics of the future Kingdom), Gospel passages (such as Mt. 5-7; 19:28; 25:31-46), Acts 3:19-21, passages in the Epistles (such as 1 Cor. 15:24-25; Eph. 1:10; Heb. 6:5), and Revelation 20:1-6. According to this special revelation the Messiah, Jesus, will restore the theocratic Kingdom of God which was on earth before man's fall but was lost through that fall. The absolute, righteous, just rule of God will be enforced worldwide. Nature will be restored to its prefall condition (Mt. 19:28; Acts 3:19-21; Rom. 8:18-23). The climate and natural elements will be controlled perfectly for the good of man (Isa. 30:23-26; Ezek. 47:1-2; Joel 2:21-26; Zech. 14:8). There will be unprecedented growth and fruitage of trees (Isa. 41:19-20; Ezek. 36:8-11, 29-30; 47:6-7, 12; Joel 2:21-26). Animals will experience great productivity (Ezek. 36:11; 47:8-10). Food will be abundant (Ps. 72:16; Isa. 30:23-24; Jer. 31:10-14; Ezek. 34:25-30; 36:29-30; Joel 2:21-26; Zech. 8:11-12). All animals will be tame and vegetarian in diet (Isa. 11:6-9; 65:25). Diseases and deformities will be abolished (Isa. 29:18; 33:24; 35:5-6). Human life will experience great longevity (Isa. 65:20-22). War will be abolished (Isa. 2:4; Mic. 4:3). Satan will not be able to instigate any activity on the earth (Rev. 20:1-3). Man will be required to submit to the righteous rule of Messiah.

Man's responsibility during the seventh dispensation will be to obey God on the basis of conscience, human government, and the theocratic rule of Christ. This responsibility will subject man to the following test: Will he obey God on the basis of these three ruling factors?

Man will fail the test of the last dispensation. Some unsaved individuals will rebel outwardly against Christ's rule during His reign (Isa. 11:3-4; 29:20-21; Jer. 31:29-30). Others will not rebel outwardly, but they will chafe inwardly. They will despise the absolute, righteous rule of Christ but will know better than to rebel outwardly. When the seventh dispensation ends and Satan is released from the abyss, these people will follow Satan in his last revolt against God's rule (Rev. 20:7-10).

This failure of great multitudes of people in spite of the perfect government and exceptional conditions of the seventh dispensation will demonstrate that the ultimate cause of man's failure and rebellion throughout history is not his external environment and circumstances but his own inward, sinful nature which rejects the rule of God and asserts self-rule.

Man's failure in conjunction with the seventh dispensation will bring God's judgment. Those people who rebel outwardly during Christ's reign will be executed (Isa. 11:3-4; 29:20-21; Jer. 31:29-30). In addition, God will crush the huge revolt which will take place immediately after the seventh dispensation by sending fire to destroy the human rebels and casting Satan into the lake of fire for everlasting torment (Rev. 20:9-10).

Key Elements Of Dispensational Theology's Exposition Of The Biblical Philosophy Of History

Earlier in this study it was noted that in order for an exposition of the biblical philosophy of history to be valid, it must contain certain necessary elements. Now that Dispensational Theology has been surveyed as a system, it is essential to determine how it deals with those necessary elements as it attempts to exposit the Bible's philosophy of history.

The first necessary element of a valid exposition is an ultimate purpose or goal for history toward the fulfillment of which all history moves. According to Dispensational Theology, the ultimate goal of history is for God to glorify Himself by demonstrating the fact that He alone is the sovereign God.

The Bible ascribes great glory to God, indicating that everything is for His glory. It calls Him "The God of glory" (Acts 7:2), "the Father of glory" (Eph. 1:17), and "the King of glory" (Ps. 24:7-10). It declares that His name is glorious and expresses the desire that the whole earth be filled with His glory (Ps. 72:18-19). Because all things are from Him, through Him, and to Him, the Bible ascribes glory to God forever (Rom. 11:36).

It is interesting to note that the Scriptures repeatedly associate the glory of God with His sovereign rule. For example, David declared,

> Wherefore, David blessed the LORD before all the congregation; and David said, Blessed be thou, LORD God of Israel, our father, forever and ever. Thine, O LORD, is the greatness, and the power, and the glory, and the victory, and the majesty; for all that is in the heaven and in the earth is thine. Thine is the kingdom, O LORD, and thou art exalted as head above all. Both riches and honor come of thee, and thou reignest over all; and in thine hand is power and might; and in thine hand it is to make great, and to give strength unto all. Now therefore, our God, we thank thee, and praise thy glorious name (1 Chr. 29:10-13).

Many other passages associate God's glory with the concepts of His Kingship, throne, Kingdom, dominion, and authority (Ps. 29:1-2, 9-10; 96:7-10; 97:1-6; 113:4-5; 115:1-3; 145:10-13; Isa. 6:1, 3, 5; Jer. 14:21; Dan. 7:14; Mt. 19:28; 25:31; 1 Tim. 1:17; Jude 25; Rev. 5:13; 7:10-12).

The Bible indicates that God is glorified through His sovereign dealings with nations (Ezek. 39:17-21), rulers (Rom. 9:17; Dan. 4:17, 34-37), Israel (Isa. 43:1, 7; 46:13; 60:1-3; Jer. 13:11), the Church (Eph. 3:20-21), and the nonelect (Rom. 9:17-18, 21). God is glorified by His sovereign act of creation (Ps. 19:1; Rev. 4:11), His sovereign acts in storms (Ps. 29:1-3, 9-10), His sovereign judgments (Isa. 2:19, 21; 59:18-19; Ezek. 39:17-21; Rev. 11:13; 19:1-2), and His sovereign act of hiding knowledge from human beings (Prov. 25:2). God glorifies Himself by sovereignly redeeming lost human beings and sovereignly keeping those whom He has redeemed (Rom. 9:23; 15:7-9; Eph. 1:5-6, 12, 14, 18; Phil. 4:19-20; 2 Tim. 4:18). God is to be glorified through the righteous deeds of believers performed through the equipment which God sovereignly gives (1 Cor. 10:31; Phil. 1:11; Heb. 13:21).

The successive dispensations glorify God in several ways. First, they demonstrate that God is the sovereign Ruler throughout history in spite of Satan's attempt to overthrow that rule and man's rebellion against it. The fact that God can hold man responsible to obey His different ways of administering His rule throughout history and can judge man for his failures to obey clearly demonstrates that God is sovereign through history. Second, the dispensations show how desperately man needs to submit to God's rule in order to have things right on earth. They display the disorder and tragedy which result from the rejection of God's rule. Third, the dispensations progressively move history toward the fulfillment of its God-intended climax. In the final "dispensation of the fullness of times" (Eph. 1:9-10), God will fully glorify Himself by crushing Satan and his kingdom (Rom. 16:20; Rev. 20:1-3), restoring His own Kingdom rule to the earth through Jesus Christ (Rev. 11:15; 20:4-6), and reversing the tragic consequences of man's rebellion (Mt. 19:28; Acts 3:19-21).

The second necessary element of a valid exposition of the Bible's philosophy of history is the recognition of distinctions or things which differ in history. Dispensational Theology asserts that distinctions are the result of God's administering His rule in different ways at different periods of history. In other words, distinctions are the result of the different dispensations of God's rule.

The third necessary element is a proper concept of the progress of revelation. Dispensational Theology states that each new dispensation, since it involves a new way of God's administering His rule of the world, requires new revelation.

The fourth necessary element is a unifying principle which ties the distinctions and progressive stages of revelation together and which directs them toward the fulfillment of the purpose of history. Dispensational Theology's unifying principle for all of history is the sovereign rule of God.

Indispensable Factors Of Dispensational Theology

Three factors are indispensable to Dispensational Theology. They clearly make Dispensational Theology distinct from Covenant Theology. Any system of theology which does not contain all three is not dispensational in the truest sense of the term.[5]

The first factor is the recognition of the distinction between the nation of Israel and the Church. As noted earlier, Covenant Theology believes that the Church existed in Old Testament times and that Israel was a major part of the Church in the Old Testament. Thus, it is convinced that Israel and the Church are essentially the same. By contrast, Dispensational Theology believes that Israel and the Church are distinct entities. It is convinced that although both have had special relationships with God, they are not essentially the same. This distinction between Israel and the Church will be dealt with more in depth in a future chapter.

The second indispensable factor is the consistent use of a single hermeneutic (a single method of interpreting the Bible) — namely, the historical-grammatical method. In this method, words are given the common, ordinary meaning which they had in the culture and time in which the passage was written. As noted earlier, Covenant Theology employs a double hermeneutic — the historical-grammatical method for many passages but also the allegorical or spiritualizing method for a number of prophetic passages dealing with the future of Israel and the future Kingdom of God. By contrast, Dispensational Theology is convinced that the historical-grammatical method should be employed for all of Scripture, including those prophetic passages related to Israel and the Kingdom of God.

The third indispensable factor is the recognition that the ultimate purpose of history is the glory of God through the demonstration that He alone is the sovereign God. As noted earlier, Covenant Theology advocates that the ultimate purpose of history is the glory of God through the redemption of the elect. By contrast, although Dispensational Theology recognizes that the redemption of elect human beings is a very important part of God's purpose for history, it is convinced that it is only one part of that purpose. During the course of history God is working out many other programs in addition to the program of redeeming people. All of these programs must be contributing something to the ultimate purpose of history. Thus, the ultimate purpose of history has to be large enough to incorporate all of God's programs, not just one of them. Dispensational Theology proposes that the glory of God through the demonstration that He alone is the sovereign God is the only purpose capable of doing this. It also is convinced that the Scriptures indicate that this is the ultimate purpose of history.

SIX

THE ABRAHAMIC COVENANT

Preliminary Considerations

I n previous chapters two major systems of theology (Covenant Theology and Dispensational Theology) have been examined in survey fashion. These two systems frequently differ from each other in their approaches to the major biblical covenants. These differences are significant, for they lead to contrasting views concerning the Millennium or future Kingdom of God foretold in the Scriptures. These differences are significant for another reason: They lead to contrasting views regarding the permanent existence of Israel as a nation and Israel's permanent ownership of the promised land. Has God promised Israel permanent existence as a nation? Has He guaranteed Israel permanent ownership of the promised land and, therefore, the right to possess that land?

A number of the biblical covenants will determine the final outcome of these important issues. Because this is so, the approach which one takes to these covenants is most crucial. In light of this fact, this and future chapters will examine the biblical covenants which relate to these issues.

Major Issues Related To The Abrahamic Covenant

The Abrahamic Covenant involves three major issues. First, does it promise Israel permanent existence as a nation?

Second, does it promise Israel permanent ownership of the promised land? Third, is the covenant conditional or unconditional? If it is conditional, the fulfillment of its promises is dependent upon the obedience of Abraham, Isaac, Jacob, and their physical descendants, the people of Israel. If the Abrahamic Covenant is unconditional, the fulfillment of its promises is dependent upon the faithfulness of God to His Word, not upon human obedience.

The Parties Of The Abrahamic Covenant

The Abrahamic Covenant was established by God with Abraham and his *physical* descendants, Isaac, Jacob, and the people of Israel. Genesis 15:18 states, "In the same day the LORD made a covenant with Abram, saying, Unto thy seed have I given this land, from the river of Egypt unto the great river, the river Euphrates." In Genesis 17:4, 6-7 God said to Abraham, "As for me, behold, my covenant is with thee...and I will make thee exceedingly fruitful,...And I will establish my covenant between me and thee and thy seed after thee in their generations for an everlasting covenant, to be a God unto thee, and to thy seed after thee."

The fact that God established the Abrahamic Covenant with the *physical* descendants of Abraham is made even more clear in Genesis 17:19, 21 where He said, "Sarah, thy wife, shall bear thee a son indeed; and thou shalt call his name Isaac: and I will establish my covenant with him for an everlasting covenant, and with his seed after him....But my covenant will I establish with Isaac, whom Sarah shall bear unto thee." God reestablished the promises of the covenant with Abraham's physical grandson, Jacob (Gen. 28:13-17; 35:9-12; 48:3-4). The instructions which Joseph, Abraham's great-grandson, gave at the end of his life clearly indicate that he understood the Abrahamic Covenant to have been made with Abraham and his *physical* descendants (Gen. 50:24-25).

The Historical Establishment
Of The Abrahamic Covenant

Although some of the promises of the Abrahamic Covenant were given by God in Genesis 12:2-3 and 13:14-17, the covenant was not formally established until Genesis 15:7-21. It is specifically stated in Genesis 15:18 that "In the same day the LORD made a covenant with Abram." God formally established the covenant in the following manner: While Abraham slept a deep sleep, God (represented by a smoking oven and a flaming torch) moved between the pieces of animals which He had commanded Abraham to cut in two. Jeremiah 34:18 makes it clear that this procedure of passing between pieces of animals was a common way of establishing covenants in Old Testament times.

The Promises Of The Abrahamic Covenant

God made three major kinds of promises in the Abrahamic Covenant. First, there were *personal promises to Abraham.* God vowed to bless Abraham and to make him a blessing to others (Gen. 12:2), to make his name great (12:2), to give him many physical descendants (13:16; 15:4-5; 17:6), to make him the father of a multitude of nations (17:4-5), to give him the land of Canaan for an everlasting possession (13:14-15, 17; 15:7; 17:8), and to bless those who blessed Abraham and curse those who cursed him (12:3).

Second, God made *national promises concerning Israel.* God promised to make a great nation of Abraham's physical descendants (12:2), to give the land of Canaan from the river of Egypt to the river Euphrates to Abraham's physical descendants forever (12:7; 13:14-15; 15:18-21; 17:8), and to give the Abrahamic Covenant to his descendants for an everlasting covenant (17:7, 19). The Genesis 17:19 passage indicates that God intended the covenant to continue on through Isaac, Abraham's literal son, and Isaac's descendants — thus, through Abraham's *physical* seed. The fact that God promised to give Abraham's physical descendants the land of Canaan *forever* and the covenant for an *everlasting* covenant demands that Israel never perish as a people. Should Israel ever perish as a nation, it could not possess the land forever, and its Abrahamic Covenant could not be everlasting.

Third, God made *universal promises which would affect all peoples of the world.* God vowed that all families of the earth would be blessed through Abraham's physical line of descent (12:3; 22:18; 28:14). As shall be seen later, great spiritual blessing has been made available to all peoples through Jesus Christ and the Jews.

In addition, Jesus' statements in Matthew 25:31-46 (especially verses 40 and 45) seem to indicate that when God promised to bless those who blessed Abraham and curse those who cursed him, He intended this to be applicable, not only to Abraham, but also to Israel. In other words, God's blessing or cursing of the peoples of the world would be determined to a large extent by their blessing or cursing of Israel. Jesus' statements in Matthew 25 promise blessing to saved Gentiles who will aid persecuted Jews of the Tribulation period and judgment to unsaved Gentiles who will not aid them.

The Partial Historic Fulfillment Of The Abrahamic Covenant

Parts of the Abrahamic Covenant have been fulfilled historically already. *Personally,* God did bless Abraham (He gave him great wealth and other blessings, Gen. 24:1, 35). God did make him a blessing to others (for example, Abraham rescued Lot from captivity, Gen. 14). God has made Abraham's name great (Judaism, Christianity, and

Islam have respected his name for centuries). God has given him many physical descendants and made him the father of a multitude of nations (Israel has descended from him through Isaac and Jacob; Arab nations have descended from him through Ishmael).

Nationally, God did make a great nation (Israel) of Abraham's physical descendants. He did give the promised land to Israel after its exodus from Egypt (Dt. 31:7-8; 32:45-52; Josh. 1:1-5, 10-11). In addition, Israel has never perished as a people.

Universally, God has made great blessing available to all families of the earth through Abraham's physical line of descent (redemption and other blessings have been provided through Jesus Christ; the Scriptures have been produced primarily by Jews). God has blessed those people and nations who have blessed Israel, and He has judged those who have abused Israel.

It should be noted that those parts of the Abrahamic Covenant which have been fulfilled thus far have been fulfilled *literally* (in accordance with the historical-grammatical method of interpreting the Bible, not in accordance with the allegorical or spiritualizing method). This would seem to indicate that God intends every promise of that covenant to be fulfilled in that manner.

In addition, it should be noted that some parts of the Abrahamic Covenant have not been fulfilled totally. Inasmuch as God promised to give the land of Canaan for an *everlasting* possession to Abraham's physical descendants (Gen. 17:8) and to give the Abrahamic Covenant for an *everlasting* covenant to those same descendants (Gen. 17:7, 19), it cannot rightly be said that all the promises of the covenant have been fulfilled totally until at least the end of world history.

The Controversy Concerning The Nature Of The Abrahamic Covenant

In many respects the most crucial of the three major issues related to the Abrahamic Covenant is if the covenant is conditional or unconditional. This issue is most crucial because it determines the outcome of the other two major issues which were noted earlier.

If the Abrahamic Covenant is *unconditional* (not dependent upon the obedience of Abraham, Isaac, Jacob, and their physical descendants, the people of Israel, for the fulfillment of its promises), then every promise of that covenant must be fulfilled including the promises that Israel would be given *forever* the land described in Genesis 15:18 and that the Abrahamic Covenant would be an *everlasting* covenant for Israel. This would mean that Israel will last forever as a people and that God has a future program for that nation and its land. It would also mean that the biblical prophecies concerning the future of Israel and its land are to be interpreted literally and that the Dispensational-Premillennial view of those prophecies is correct.

By contrast, if the Abrahamic Covenant is *conditional* (dependent upon the obedience of Abraham, Isaac, Jacob, and the people of Israel for the fulfillment of its promises), then not every promise of that covenant has to be fulfilled. Disobedience by Abraham, Isaac, Jacob, or the people of Israel could nullify the fulfillment of the covenant's promises. In light of such disobedience, Israel would not have to be given the land of Canaan *forever*, the Abrahamic Covenant would not have to be an *everlasting* covenant for Israel, the biblical prophecies concerning the future of Israel and its land could be interpreted allegorically or spiritualized, and the Dispensational-Premillennial view of those prophecies would be wrong.

Theologians disagree concerning whether the Abrahamic Covenant is conditional or unconditional. Dispensational Theologians contend that the covenant is unconditional. Covenant Theologians disagree with each other on this issue. Many Covenant Theologians say that the Abrahamic Covenant is conditional, while others say that it is unconditional but that the national promises to Israel must be interpreted allegorically, not literally.

Those who believe that the Abrahamic Covenant is conditional point to certain biblical statements as their proof. For example, Genesis 17:1-2 declares that when Abraham was 99 years old, God spoke to him, "walk before me, and be thou perfect. And I will make my covenant between me and thee, and will multiply thee exceedingly." In Genesis 22:16-18 God said to Abraham,

> By myself have I sworn, saith the LORD; for because thou hast done this thing, and hast not withheld thy son, thine only son; That in blessing I will bless thee, and in multiplying I will multiply thy seed as the stars of the heaven, and as the sand which is upon the seashore; and thy seed shall possess the gate of his enemies; And in thy seed shall all the nations of the earth be blessed, because thou hast obeyed my voice.

In Genesis 26:3-5 God said to Isaac,

> Sojourn in this land, and I will be with thee, and will bless thee; for unto thee, and unto thy seed, I will give all these countries, and I will perform the oath which I swore unto Abraham thy father; And I will make thy seed to multiply as the stars of heaven, and will give unto thy seed all these countries; and in thy seed shall all the nations of the earth be blessed; Because that Abraham obeyed

> my voice, and kept my charge, my commandments,
> my statutes, and my laws.

On the surface, these statements appear to indicate that the Abrahamic Covenant is conditional in nature. Before that conclusion is drawn, however, two significant things should be noted. First, these statements were made years after God formally established the covenant with Abraham in Genesis 15. When the covenant was formally established, God stated no conditions. According to Galatians 3:15, once a covenant has been established no conditions are added to it. Thus, to say that the statements of Genesis 17:1-2, 22:16-18, and 26:3-5 indicate that the Abrahamic Covenant is conditional is to say that God added conditions after the covenant was established and that God thereby violated the principle of Galatians 3:15.

Second, when the covenant was formally established, only God passed between the halves of the animals. A deep sleep came upon Abraham so that he could not move between them. This indicated that the fulfillment of the covenant's promises was totally dependent upon God, not upon Abraham. The only time that both parties of a covenant would pass between the pieces of animals was when the fulfillment of the covenant was dependent upon both parties keeping commitments. Concerning the significance of God alone moving between the halves of the animals, Berry wrote,

> Here it is to be noted that it is a smoking furnace and a flaming torch, representing God, not Abraham, which passed between the pieces. Such an act, it would seem, should be shared by both parties, but in this case it is doubtless to be explained by the fact that the covenant is principally a promise by Jeh. He is the one who binds Himself.[1]

Third, God formally established the Abrahamic covenant in response to Abraham's question, "Lord GOD, whereby shall I know that I shall inherit it [the land]?" (Gen. 15:8). In the immediate context (v. 7) God had just reminded Abraham of the fact that He had brought him out of Ur of the Chaldeans in order to give him the land of Canaan to possess it. In response to this reminder, Abraham asked God for confirming proof that He would fulfill His promise to give him the land. God consented to give such proof and formally established a solemn covenant with Abraham as that proof. The point is that the purpose for the formal establishment of the Abrahamic Covenant was that of assuring Abraham that God would keep *His* word. The total focus of the covenant was the faithfulness of God to *His* commitment. The focus had nothing to do with the faithfulness or obedience of Abraham or his physical descendants. If the fulfillment of the promises of the Abrahamic Covenant depended in any way at all upon the faithfulness of anyone other than God, how could that covenant accomplish its intended purpose?

Fourth, the Abrahamic Covenant was still in effect even after the patriarchs of Israel had sinned several times. Although Abraham had sinned several times (Gen. 16:20) after the covenant had been established, God later confirmed the covenant with his son, Isaac (Gen. 26:1-4). In spite of Isaac's sin after that confirmation (Gen. 26:6-11), God later confirmed the covenant with his son, Jacob (Gen. 28:13-15; 35:9-12; 48:3-4). Even though Jacob and his sons were guilty of various sins (Gen. 37:18-36; 38:12-26), Joseph regarded the covenant to be in effect at the end of his life and was convinced that it would continue to be so into the future (Gen. 50:24-26). Several generations after Joseph, when the people of Israel were enslaved in Egypt, God made it clear to Moses that the Abrahamic Covenant was still in effect (Ex. 2:24; 6:2-8).

Fifth, even after the nation of Israel had sinned in numerous ways over the course of several centuries, David regarded the Abrahamic Covenant to be in effect with Israel in his day. In 1 Chronicles 16:15-18 David exhorted the Jews,

> Be ye mindful always of his covenant; the word which he commanded to a thousand generations, Even of the covenant which he made with Abraham, and of his oath unto Isaac, And hath confirmed the same to Jacob for a law, and to Israel for an everlasting covenant, Saying, Unto thee will I give the land of Canaan, the lot of your inheritance (cf. Ps. 105:8-11).

Why would David exhort Jews of his day to *be mindful* of the Abrahamic Covenant if it were no longer in effect with them? Why would he exhort Jews to remember the covenant *always*, and why would he specifically call attention to the promise concerning Israel's possession of the land if at any point in history that promise of the covenant could be annulled?

Sixth, Moses promised that even though Israel would become idolatrous and evil and would be scattered and suffer because of its sin, in the latter days it would have opportunity to return to God and be obedient *because* God would not fail Israel, nor destroy it, nor forget the Abrahamic Covenant which He swore to their fathers (Dt. 4:25-31). Several things should be noted concerning this promise. First, it is the same people (literal Israel, the physical descendants of Abraham) who would depart from God and be scattered from the land of Canaan (v. 26) who would also have the opportunity to return to Him and be obedient in the latter days. This implies that the literal nation of Israel will still exist in the latter days and that God will have a program for that nation during that period of history. Second, the Abrahamic Covenant would still be in effect with the literal nation of Israel in the latter days in spite of its idolatry, evil, and traumatic history of dispersion and suffering. Certainly that could not be true if the continuation of that covenant with Israel were dependent upon the faithfulness or obedience of that nation. Third, Moses made it clear (v. 31) that this promise in Deuteronomy 4 would continue to be in effect because of *God's* faithfulness. Even though Israel would fail Him, He would not fail it. He would be faithful to His covenant commitment which he had sworn to Abraham, Isaac, and Jacob.

Seventh, even after Israel had compiled its sordid record of sin throughout all its centuries of Old Testament history, the Holy Spirit indicated that the Abrahamic Covenant was still in effect with that nation and that that covenant had something to do with Israel's deliverance from its enemies (Lk. 1:67-75). Shortly before Jesus' birth the Holy Spirit prophesied through the Jewish priest, Zacharias,

> Blessed be the Lord God of Israel; for he hath visited and redeemed his people, And hath raised up an horn of salvation for us in the house of his servant, David;...That we should be saved from our enemies, and from the hand of all that hate us; To perform the mercy promised to our fathers, and to remember his holy covenant; The oath which he swore to our father, Abraham, That he would grant unto us that we, being delivered out of the hand of our enemies, might serve him without fear.

Eighth, even though Israel committed its ultimate sin of rejecting the Son of God, Jesus, as its Messiah, the Apostle Peter still regarded the Jews (even the very Jews who had rejected Christ) as children of the Abrahamic Covenant. Peter said to a crowd in Jerusalem,

> Ye men of Israel,...The God of Abraham, and of Isaac, and of Jacob, The God of our fathers, hath glorified his Son, Jesus, whom ye delivered up and denied in the presence of Pilate, when he was determined to let him go. But ye denied the Holy One and the Just, and desired a murderer to be granted unto you; And killed the Prince of life, whom God hath raised from the dead, of which we are witnesses (Acts 3:12-15).

Having thereby identified his audience, Peter said to them,

> Ye are the sons of the prophets, and of the covenant which God made with our fathers, saying unto Abraham, And in thy seed shall all the kindreds of the earth be blessed. Unto you first God, having raised up his Son, Jesus, sent him to bless you, in turning away every one of you from his iniquities (Acts 3:25-26).

Peter's use of the present tense ("are the sons") indicates his conviction that these Jews were still sons of the covenant and that the covenant was still in effect with them. The only way the Abrahamic Covenant could still be in effect with the nation of Israel after its rejection of Christ was if that covenant were unconditional. If that covenant had been dependent upon the obedience of Israel for the fulfillment of its promises, certainly it would have been nullified by Israel's worst sin.

Ninth, the Epistle to the Hebrews indicates that God doubly emphasized the fact that the Abrahamic Covenant was His *unchangeable purpose* and that, therefore, that covenant was still to be a source of encouragement to Jews who were living when that epistle was written. Hebrews 6:13-18 states,

> For when God made promise to Abraham, because he could swear by no greater, he swore by himself, Saying, Surely, blessing I will bless thee, and multiplying I will multiply thee...For men verily swear by the greater, and an oath for confirmation is to them an end of all strife. Wherein God, willing more abundantly to show unto the heirs of promise the immutability of his counsel, confirmed it by an oath, That by two immutable things, in which it was impossible for God to lie, we might have a strong consolation, who have fled for refuge to lay hold upon the hope set before us.

Two things should be noted concerning this statement. First, God wanted to impress Abraham and his descendants with the fact that He is absolutely determined to fulfill the Abrahamic Covenant and that fulfillment of the covenant is dependent totally upon God's faithfulness to His Word. Second, the Abrahamic Covenant was still to be a source of encouragement to Jews who were living when Hebrews was written (during the 60s A.D.), in spite of the fact that Israel had rejected Christ several decades earlier.

Tenth, the Abrahamic Covenant included a universal promise of blessing to all families of the earth through Abraham's seed. The fulfillment of this promise involved the coming of the Redeemer and the provision of salvation for all peoples of the world. If the Abrahamic Covenant were conditional, then the coming of the Redeemer and the provision of salvation were dependent upon the obedience of Abraham, Isaac, Jacob, and the people of Israel. Such an arrangement would have jeopardized the coming of Christ and the whole program of redemption. It also would have undermined the certainty of fulfillment of many Old Testament messianic prophecies. It is a fact, however, that the Redeemer did come and salvation was provided in spite of the many centuries of disobedience by Abraham, Isaac, Jacob, and the people of Israel. That fact practically demands that the Abrahamic Covenant be unconditional in nature. And if it is unconditional in nature, then the fulfillment of *all* its promises (including the national promises to literal Israel) is dependent totally upon the faithfulness of God to His Word.

SEVEN

THE EFFECTS OF THE ABRAHAMIC COVENANT UPON ISRAEL

The Guarantee Of Israel's Permanent Existence As A Nation

I n light of its unconditional nature, the Abrahamic Covenant has at least a twofold effect upon Israel. First, *it guarantees Israel permanent existence as a nation.* Since the Abrahamic Covenant is an unconditional covenant (totally dependent upon God's faithfulness for fulfillment), and since God declared it to be an everlasting covenant with the people of Israel (Gen. 17:7, 19; 1 Chr. 16:15-17; Ps. 105:8-10), the nation of Israel must exist forever. A covenant cannot be everlasting if one party of the covenant ceases to exist.

Several biblical passages promise that in spite of Israel's terrible sins, it never will be totally destroyed as a nation. In Deuteronomy 4:25-31 Moses declared to the Israelites,

When thou shalt beget children, and children's children, and ye shall have remained long in the land, and shall corrupt yourselves, and make a carved image, or the likeness of anything, and shall do evil in the sight of the LORD thy God, to provoke him to anger, I call heaven and earth to witness against you this day, that ye shall soon utterly perish from off the land whereunto ye go over the Jordan to possess it; ye shall not prolong your days upon it, but shall utterly be destroyed. And the

LORD shall scatter you among the nations, and ye shall be left few in number among the nations, where the LORD shall lead you. And there ye shall serve gods, the work of men's hands, wood and stone, which neither see, nor hear, nor eat, nor smell. But if from there thou shalt seek the LORD thy God, thou shalt find him, if thou seek him with all thy heart and with all thy soul. When thou art in tribulation, and all these things are come upon thee, even in the latter days, if thou turn to the LORD thy God, and shalt be obedient unto his voice (For the LORD thy God is a merciful God), he will not forsake thee, neither destroy thee, nor forget the covenant of thy fathers which he swore unto them.

At first glance verses 26 and 31 appear to contradict each other. Verse 26 states that Israel will be utterly destroyed, but verse 31 declares that God will not destroy Israel. It is important to note that the words translated *destroy* in these verses are two different words with two different meanings. Certainly the word *destroyed* in verse 26 cannot mean *to put out of existence,* for the next several verses indicate that these same people would be scattered among the nations, serve false gods, and have opportunity to seek the Lord *after* they had been destroyed. Nonexisting people cannot perform such activities. The context requires that *destroyed* of verse 26 be understood as *overthrow* or *remove from the land.*

In verse 26 God warned that He would remove the nation of Israel from its land because of its terrible sins, but in verse 31 He promised that He would not destroy the nation of Israel in the sense of putting it out of existence. God will chasten the nation, but He will never annihilate it for its sins. Thus, verses 26 and 31 do not contradict each other.

It is significant that God linked His promise not to destroy the nation of Israel with His promises not to fail Israel or forget the Abrahamic Covenant which He swore to Israel's ancestors (v. 31). The implication is that Israel's permanent existence as a nation is guaranteed through the Abrahamic Covenant, because that covenant is totally dependent upon the faithfulness of God for its fulfillment.

God made a similar promise to the nation of Israel in Jeremiah 30:11:

> For I am with thee, saith the LORD, to save thee; though I make a full end of all nations to which I have scattered thee, yet will I not make a full end of thee, but I will correct thee in measure, and will not leave thee altogether unpunished.

In Jeremiah 46:27-28 God declared,

> But fear not, O my servant, Jacob, and be not dismayed, O Israel; for, behold, I will save thee from afar off, and thy seed from the land of their captivity; and Jacob shall return, and be in rest and at ease, and none shall make him afraid. Fear thou not, O Jacob, my servant, saith the LORD; for I am with thee; for I will make a full end of all the nations to which I have driven thee; but I will not make a full end of thee, but correct thee in measure; yet will I not leave thee wholly unpunished.

In Amos 9:8 God promised, "I will not utterly destroy the house of Jacob."

In Romans 11 Paul taught that even in his day (after Israel's rejection of Christ and while they were enemies of the gospel) the people of Israel were still beloved of God in accordance with His sovereign choice of them to be His special people (vv. 1-2, 28) and for the sake of their ancestors to whom God swore the Abrahamic Covenant (v. 28). If God were to reject Israel or allow it to perish totally as a nation from the earth, He would thereby violate His own sovereign choice and betray Abraham, Isaac, and Jacob. In light of this, Paul declared that God's calling of Israel to be His special people is irrevocable (v. 29).

The Guarantee Of Israel's Permanent Ownership Of The Land

The second major effect which the Abrahamic Covenant has upon Israel is that *it guarantees Israel permanent ownership of the promised land.* Since the Abrahamic Covenant is an unconditional covenant, and since one of God's promises in that covenant was to give the land of Canaan to Abraham and the people of Israel *forever* (Gen. 12:7; 13:14-15; 15:18-21; 17:8; 1 Chr. 16:15-18; Ps. 105:8-11), Israel must hold ownership of Canaan through the end of history. This does not mean that Israel had *to live* in this land continuously in order to maintain ownership. Many landlords own property which they do not personally inhabit; thus, ownership does not require personal inhabiting of property by its owner. Israel's dispersions from Canaan because of sins have not ended its ownership of the land; therefore, Israel has rightful claim to the land both today and in the future.

In line with this rightful claim, many of the prophets foretold a total, permanent restoration of the people of Israel to the land which God promised to their fathers and them in the Abrahamic Covenant: "Thy people also shall all be righteous; they shall inherit the land forever, the branch of my planting, the work of my hands, that I may be glorified" (Isa. 60:21).

Jeremiah foretold that in the future, when Jerusalem becomes "the throne of the LORD" and all nations are gathered to it, all the tribes of Israel will be reunited in the land which God gave to their fathers as an inheritance (Jer. 3:17-18). Again he declared that when David's righteous Branch, the Messiah, reigns as King, God will regather the sons of Israel from the nations of the world and restore them to their own land which He gave to their fathers (Jer. 16:14-15; 23:5-8; 30:3). Further, through Jeremiah God promised that when He restores Israel to the land, He will make the Israelites dwell in safety, will do them good, and "will plant them in this assuredly" with all His heart and soul (Jer. 32:37, 41). The language of this promise indicates that God is fervently committed to this future restoration of Israel to its land and that this restoration is dependent upon God's faithfulness to His Word expressed in the Abrahamic Covenant.

Ezekiel prophesied that God will restore all the sons of Israel to their own land, the land which He swore to give to their forefathers. At that time God will make Israel one nation; no longer will it be divided into two kingdoms. Israel will have one king. The Israelites will live securely in their land. No longer will they be a prey to other nations or have to endure their insults, for God will execute judgments upon all who scorn them. The Israelites and their descendants will live in their own land forever. Never again will they be the victims of famine or wild beasts. God will not hide His face from them any longer. He will make an everlasting peace covenant with them, in spite of Israel's evil, corrupt ways, and in spite of the fact that the nation does not deserve it: "I do not this for your sakes, O house of Israel, but for mine holy name's sake" (Ezek. 36:22). He will do it to vindicate the holiness of His name, to make Israel recognize their true God, and to impress all the other nations with Himself (Ezek. 20:42, 44; 28:25-26; 34:13, 27-29; 36:22-32; 37:11-26; 39:25-29). These divinely stated purposes indicate once again that Israel's future, permanent restoration to its own land is ultimately dependent upon God, not upon Israel's obedience.

The Prophet Amos declared that God will restore the captivity of Israel. At that time the Israelites will rebuild their ruined cities, plant vineyards and gardens, and enjoy the fruit of their labors. Amos quoted the following declaration of God: "And I will plant them upon their land, and they shall no more be pulled up out of their land which I have given them" (Amos 9:15).

Several observations should be made on the basis of these prophetic passages. The present restoration of Israel to the homeland which began in the middle of the 20th century is not the fulfillment of these prophecies. Several things indicate this. First, these prophecies foretell a total restoration of the Jews to their land from all the nations of the world. By contrast, the 20th century restoration has not been total. Those Jews who are still scattered among the nations of the world are several times more numerous than those who live in the state of Israel. In fact, the United States alone has several million more Jewish residents than the state of Israel. In addition, because of severe economic conditions in Israel, more Jews are leaving their homeland to return to the nations of the world than there are Jews entering it.

Second, these prophetic passages indicate that when this future restoration of Israel to the homeland takes place, all the Jews will be righteous. They will dwell securely in complete safety. They will no longer endure the insults of the nations. No one will make them afraid. The Messiah, the righteous Branch of David, will reign over them as their King. They will recognize their true God. By contrast, none of these things is a reality for the Jews in the present state of Israel. These conditions will not become a reality for Israel until the Messiah comes in His Second Coming to reign as King. Thus, the restoration of Israel foretold in these prophetic passages will not take place until His Second Coming.

Another observation to be made on the basis of these prophetic passages is that the divine promises of these passages indicate that God regards the nation of Israel as the continuous owner of the land of Canaan in spite of its various dispersions from that land. They indicate this by God's use of such expressions as *their own land*. God punished Israel for its sins by removing it temporarily from its own land, but He will never punish it to the extent of abolishing its ownership of that land. To do so would be to violate His promise in the Abrahamic Covenant to give the land of Canaan to the fathers and people of Israel *forever*.

There is, then, an inseparable link between the Abrahamic Covenant and the prophetic passages which promise Israel's total, permanent restoration to its homeland and future blessing. The covenant is the foundation or basis for these prophetic passages, and the passages are the natural outgrowth or result of the covenant. They foretell the ultimate, final fulfillment of the divine promise to Israel contained in the Abrahamic Covenant.

Some Important Conclusions

Earlier it was noted that the unconditional nature of the Abrahamic Covenant causes it to have a twofold effect upon Israel. This twofold effect leads to some important conclusions.

One effect is the fact that the Abrahamic Covenant guarantees Israel permanent existence as a nation, which leads to the conclusion that Jews will always be present in the world. No matter how ugly and powerful anti-Semitism may become, it will never be able to annihilate the Jews totally. This guarantee of the Abrahamic Covenant stands as an unyielding, immovable stone against which anti-Semitism will dash itself to bits in the future Tribulation period when it makes its last and greatest effort to destroy Israel. This guarantee also explains the reason for the continued existence of the Jews today in spite of the repeated persecutions and attempts at genocide made against their nation throughout history.

The second effect is the fact that the Abrahamic Covenant guarantees Israel permanent ownership of the land of Canaan. Certainly an owner of property has the right to occupy it at any time while he owns it. This effect leads to the conclusion that Israel has the right to occupy that land at any time, even those times when world conditions do not permit it to do so. This leads to the further conclusion that since the land which the state of Israel now occupies in the Middle East is part of the land which God gave to Israel permanently in the Abrahamic Covenant, the 20th century state of Israel has the right to occupy that land today and to exist there as an independent nation. Even if future world events should force Israel out of its homeland again, that would not indicate that God has revoked that nation's right to occupy that land. When God judged Israel by scattering it from its land after it rejected its Messiah, Jesus, He regarded that scattering as a temporary loss of occupancy, not a termination of ownership for Israel. From God's viewpoint, those people who took over occupancy of the land after Israel was scattered did not become the owners of the land. God permitted them and their descendants to use that land temporarily as squatters, but He did not give them right or title to do so. Thus, when the modern state of Israel drove these people out, it was not dispossessing them of land which they rightfully owned. Instead, it was removing them from land which they had temporarily squatted upon. Certainly one's heart goes out to those people who were so removed because of the hardships their removal has caused, but the Abrahamic Covenant indicates that Israel has the right to occupy its own land today.

EIGHT

THE PALESTINIAN OR DEUTERONOMIC COVENANT

The Background Of The Covenant

T wo significant things should be observed concerning the Palestinian Covenant. The first is the *background of the covenant.* The Palestinian Covenant was established by God with Israel after the establishment of the Mosaic Covenant, and it was separate from the Mosaic Covenant. Deuteronomy 29:1 states, "These are the words of the covenant, which the LORD commanded Moses to make with the children of Israel in the land of Moab, beside the covenant which he made with them in Horeb." (A comparison of Exodus 19 and 20 with Deuteronomy 5 indicates that Horeb and Sinai are two different names for the same mountain, the mountain where God established the Mosaic Covenant with Israel.)

In preparation for the establishment of the Palestinian Covenant, God made promises of blessing and cursing to the nation of Israel. In Deuteronomy 28:1-14 God promised that if Israel obeyed the Mosaic Law, He would bless the nation abundantly and make it the head nation of the world. But then God warned that if Israel disobeyed the Mosaic Law, He would curse the nation abundantly with such things as drought, famine, pestilence, foreign oppression, captivity, and worldwide dispersion (Dt. 28:15-68).

Having given these preparatory promises, God entered into the Palestinian Covenant relationship with Israel. In Deuteronomy 29:10-13 Moses said to Israel,

Ye stand this day, all of you, before the LORD your God: your captains of your tribes, your elders, and your officers, with all the men of Israel, Your little ones, your wives, and thy sojourner who is in thy camp, from the hewer of thy wood unto the drawer of thy water; That thou shouldest enter into covenant with the LORD thy God, and into his oath, which the LORD thy God maketh with thee this day; That he may establish thee today for a people unto himself, and that he may be unto thee a God, as he hath said unto thee, and as he hath sworn unto thy fathers, to Abraham, to Isaac, and to Jacob.

God established the Palestinian Covenant at the end of Israel's 40 years of wilderness wandering, just a short time before the nation was to invade Canaan (Dt. 29:5-8). The place of its establishment was the land of Moab (Dt. 29:1), east of the Dead Sea across from the land of Canaan. The parties of the covenant were God, the new generation of Israelites which was to invade Canaan, and succeeding generations of the nation. In Deuteronomy 29:14-15 Moses said to Israel, "Neither with you only do I make this covenant and this oath, But with him who standeth here with us this day before the LORD our God, and also with him who is not here with us this day." As a new generation was about to begin a new chapter in Israel's history, it had to be reminded in a solemn way of Israel's special covenant relationship with Jehovah. This reminder appears to have been the purpose of the Palestinian Covenant.

The Promises Of The Covenant

The second major thing to be observed concerning the Palestinian Covenant is that in conjunction with the establishment of the covenant God made *very significant promises to Israel* (Dt. 30:1-10). Moses indicated that these promises will be fulfilled *when all* the blessings and curses promised in Deuteronomy 28 have been fulfilled and *when* Israel genuinely returns to God and obeys Him:

> And it shall come to pass, when all these things are come upon thee, the blessing and the curse, which I have set before thee, and thou shalt call them to mind among all the nations, to which the LORD thy God hath driven thee, And shalt return unto the LORD thy God, and shalt obey his voice according to all that I command thee this day, thou and thy children, with all thine heart, and with all thy soul (Dt. 30:1-2).

First, God promised to gather the scattered Israelites from all over the world:

> That then the LORD thy God will turn thy captivity, and have compassion upon thee, and will return and gather thee from all the nations where the LORD thy God hath scattered thee. If any of thine be driven out unto the outmost parts of heaven, from there will the LORD thy God gather thee, and from there will he fetch thee (vv. 3-4).

Second, God promised to restore the Israelites to the land of their ancestors: "And the LORD thy God will bring thee into the land which thy fathers possessed, and thou shalt possess it; and he will do thee good, and multiply thee above thy fathers" (v. 5).

Third, God promised to regenerate the Israelites of that time and their descendants, thereby causing them to love Him totally: "And the LORD thy God will circumcise thine heart, and the heart of thy seed, to love the LORD thy God with all thine heart, and with all thy soul, that thou mayest live" (v. 6). Circumcision of the heart is the Old Testament designation for regeneration (cf. Rom. 2:29).

Fourth, God promised to judge Israel's enemies: "And the LORD thy God will put all these curses upon thine enemies, and on them who hate thee, who persecuted thee" (v. 7).

Fifth, God promised that the Israelites of that time will obey Him: "And thou shalt return and obey the voice of the LORD, and do all his commandments which I command thee this day" (v. 8).

Sixth, God promised to prosper those Israelites greatly: "And the LORD thy God will make thee plenteous in every work of thine hand, in the fruit of thy body, and in the fruit of thy cattle, and in the fruit of thy land, for good; for the LORD will again rejoice over thee for good, as he rejoiced over thy fathers" (v. 9).

Centuries after God made these promises of the Palestinian Covenant to Israel, He repeated a number of them to later generations of Israelites through the Prophets Jeremiah (32:36-44) and Ezekiel (36:22-38) [see the earlier study concerning the effects of the Abrahamic Covenant upon Israel].

The Significance Of The Promises

Several significant things should be noted concerning the promises of the Palestinian Covenant. First, God made these promises to *the same national group which He later banished through dispersion to other nations* because of disobedience to Him (Dt. 28:15-68; 29:24-29; 30:1, 3). In other words, God made these promises specifically to the literal nation of Israel, including all 12 tribes (Dt. 29:10). Thus, these promises are to be fulfilled with literal Israel.

Second, these promises indicate that God always leaves the way open for unfaithful Israel to be reconciled to Him (cf. Ezek. 16). God never has and never will permanently terminate His special relationship with literal Israel.

Third, the ultimate fulfillment of these promises with Israel is still future. Moses indicated that fulfillment will not take place until all the curse of Deuteronomy 28 has been completed and Israel has genuinely returned to God and obeyed Him (Dt. 30:1-3). It is a fact that literal Israel has not yet returned to God as a nation and is not now obeying Him. In addition, in light of such things as the Holocaust of World War II and the present persecution of Jews in the Soviet Union, it is evident that all the curse of Deuteronomy 28 has not yet been completed for Israel even in this present century.

Fourth, the fact that God intends to fulfill these promises with Israel *when all* the curse of Deuteronomy 28 has been completed with that nation indicates that literal Israel will survive all of its God-ordained curse. This, therefore, is another guarantee of Israel's permanent existence as a nation. God has chastened Israel severely for centuries because of its unfaithfulness to Him, but He will never destroy its existence as a nation.

Fifth, the fact that God promised to restore literal Israel to the land (which He gave to their ancestors) *when all* the curse of Deuteronomy 28 has been fulfilled is another guarantee to Israel's permanent ownership of that land. Even though Israel has been dispersed outside Canaan for much of its history because of its disobedience to God, it has never lost its God-given ownership of that land.

Sixth, the promises of the Palestinian Covenant guarantee that literal Israel will repent and become saved in the future. God indicated that, *when all* the curse of Deuteronomy 28 has been fulfilled (when He has completed His program of chastening Israel), the Israelites will return to Him and obey Him (Dt. 30:1-2), and He will regenerate them (Dt. 30:6). Centuries after Moses spoke these promises of Israel's future repentance and salvation, other great spokesmen of God repeated them.

The Prophet Hosea declared that the sons of Israel would remain without king or prince and sacrifice for many days. However, they "shall...return, and seek the LORD, their God, and David, their king, and shall fear the LORD and his goodness in the latter days" (Hos. 3:5).

The Prophet Zechariah indicated that the same national group which would have Messiah crucified would later repent and become saved: "they shall look upon me whom they have pierced, and they shall mourn for him, as one mourneth for his only son, and shall be in bitterness for him, as one that is in bitterness for his first-born" (Zech. 12:10). Zechariah taught that God will cleanse Israel from its sin in response to this repentance: "In that day there shall be a fountain opened to the house of David and to the inhabitants of Jerusalem for sin and for uncleanness" (Zech. 13:1).

Years after Messiah's death, resurrection, and ascension the Apostle Paul taught that Israel's repentance and salvation will take place at Messiah's Second Coming:

> blindness in part is happened to Israel, until the fullness of the Gentiles be come in. And so all Israel shall be saved; as it is written, There shall come out of Zion the Deliverer, and shall turn away ungodliness from Jacob; For this is my covenant unto them, when I shall take away their sins" (Rom. 11:25-27).

Paul continued by indicating that even though the people of Israel are enemies of the gospel during this present dispensation, on the basis of God's sovereign choice He continues to love them for the sake of their fathers to whom He made covenant commitments. God's past calling of Israel to be a special people to Him is irrevocable. As a result, He will be merciful to them in the future (Rom. 11:28-32).

Thus, the promises of the Palestinian Covenant will be fulfilled in conjunction with Messiah's glorious Second Coming to earth at the end of the future Tribulation period. The Tribulation period will be the last and most terrible segment of the curse of Deuteronomy 28 upon Israel. It will be God's instrument to break Israel's rebellion and bring that nation back to Himself.

NINE

THE DAVIDIC COVENANT

The Content Of The Covenant

After David had become firmly established as king over the entire nation of Israel (2 Sam. 7:1), he expressed the desire to build a permanent house of worship for God in Jerusalem (2 Sam. 7:2-3). Through Nathan, the prophet, God revealed that it would be Solomon, David's son, and not David himself who would build the house of worship (2 Sam. 7:4-7, 12-13). Although God did not allow David to build the Temple, He did establish a significant covenant with him. Because God made this covenant with David, theologians have called it the Davidic Covenant. This covenant has special significance concerning the future Kingdom of God foretold in the Bible.

The content of the Davidic Covenant is recorded in 2 Samuel 7:8-16. Although this passage does not call God's promises to David a covenant, other passages clearly indicate that God was establishing a covenant with His servant (2 Sam. 23:5; 2 Chr. 7:18; 21:7; Ps. 89:3-4, 28-29, 34-37; Jer. 33:19-26).

In the Davidic Covenant, God made promises concerning the nation of Israel (vv. 10-11), Solomon (vv. 12-15), and David (v. 16). The promises of most importance to this study are the ones concerning David. God made three major promises with regard to David.

First, God promised, "thine house...shall be established forever before thee" (v. 16). The term *house* referred to David's physical line of descent. Thus, God was promising that David's line of descent would endure forever. In line with this divine pledge, God declared in Psalm 89, "I have made a covenant with my chosen, I have sworn unto David, my servant: Thy seed will I establish forever" (vv. 3-4). Again He said, "His seed also will I make to endure forever" (v. 29), and "His seed shall endure forever" (v. 36). Even when David's descendant, Jehoram, did evil as the king of Judah, "the LORD would not destroy the house of David, because of the covenant that he had made with David" (2 Chr. 21:7).

The second major promise God made to David was, "thy kingdom shall be established forever before thee" (v. 16). God thereby pledged that David's kingdom would never pass away permanently, even though it might not function at all times. It is a fact of history that David's kingdom has not functioned at all times since God made this solemn promise, but this divine pledge was a guarantee that David's kingdom would always have the potential of being restored to full function.

Because of this guarantee of the Davidic Covenant, Jews who lived centuries after David's kingdom had ceased to function clung to the hope of that kingdom's restoration. Thus, when Jesus made His triumphal entry into Jerusalem on Palm Sunday, throngs of Jews cried out, "Blessed be the kingdom of our father, David, that cometh in the name of the Lord" (Mk. 11:10), and when Jesus was ready to ascend to Heaven, His disciples asked if He would restore the kingdom again at that time (Acts 1:6).

The third Davidic Covenant promise concerning David was, "thy throne shall be established forever" (v. 16). Other statements concerning David's throne (2 Sam. 3:10; 1 Ki. 1:37, 47) lead to the conclusion that this is a reference to the ruling authority which David exercised as king. Thus, God pledged that the ruling authority which David exercised would never pass away permanently, even though it might not be exercised at all times. Once again it is a fact of history that David's ruling authority has not been exercised at all times since God made this solemn promise, but this divine pledge was a guarantee that David's ruling authority would always have the potential of being restored to full exercise. To put it another way, it was a guarantee that a royal descendant of David would always be available to exercise that authority when circumstances would so permit. This is indicated by God's statement to Solomon, "I have covenanted with David, thy father, saying, There shall not fail thee a man to be ruler in Israel" (2 Chr. 7:18). God also declared that He had sworn to build up David's throne "to all generations" (Ps. 89:3-4).

Because of this guarantee of the Davidic Covenant, several centuries after David's ruling authority stopped being exercised the angel Gabriel could declare concerning David's descendant, Jesus, "the Lord God shall give unto him the throne of his father, David. And he shall reign over the house of Jacob forever" (Lk. 1:32-33). The very fact that Gabriel could make such a promise clearly indicates that even though David's ruling authority had been inactive for several centuries, it had not passed away permanently.

It should be noted that God stated no conditions in the content of the Davidic Covenant when He established it with David. This indicates that the Davidic Covenant is unconditional in nature. It depends totally upon the faithfulness of God for the fulfillment of its promises.

The Major Issues Of The David Covenant

Matthew recorded the fact that Jesus Christ is "the son of David" (Mt. 1:1). Both Matthew and Luke presented genealogies which traced Jesus' ancestry back to David (Mt. 1; Lk. 3). These genealogies indicated that Jesus Christ is a physical descendant of David.

The angel Gabriel announced that God would give Jesus the throne of His ancestor, David, that Jesus would reign over the house of Jacob forever, and that Jesus' kingdom would never end (Lk. 1:31-33).

Peter declared that God had sworn with an oath to David "that of the fruit of his loins, according to the flesh, he would raise up Christ to sit on his throne" (Acts 2:30).

Isaiah prophesied concerning the Messiah, "Of the increase of his government and peace there shall be no end, upon the throne of David, and upon his kingdom, to order it, and to establish it with justice and with righteousness from henceforth even forever" (Isa. 9:7).

In light of these significant factors, both amillennial (those who say that Christ will not reign over a literal, earthly, political kingdom on this present earth) and premillennial (those who say that Christ will reign over a literal, earthly, political kingdom on this present earth *after* His Second Coming) Bible scholars agree that God's three major promises concerning David in the Davidic Covenant are fulfilled ultimately in Jesus Christ. But Amillennialists and Premillennialists disagree concerning when and how those promises are fulfilled in Him. This disagreement indicates that the *major issues* related to the Davidic Covenant are *when* and *how* God's promises concerning David are to be fulfilled in Jesus Christ.

Premillennialists believe that Christ *will* fulfill these promises in the *future* when He returns to earth in His Second Coming and then establishes and reigns over a *literal, earthly, political kingdom* for 1,000 years *on this present earth* and for eternity *on the new eternal earth.*

By contrast, some Amillennialists believe that Christ fulfills these promises *now* (during this age *before* His Second

Coming) in His *present* rule over *the Church* or *human hearts* as He sits at God's right hand on the throne of God in Heaven. According to this view, the kingdom over which Christ rules in fulfillment of the Davidic Covenant is solely *a spiritual kingdom*. It is not a literal, earthly, political kingdom. In addition, in order to be consistent, this view must equate the throne of David with the throne of God in Heaven.

Other Amillennialists believe that Christ will fulfill these promises in *eternity future* after the present earth has been destroyed and history is concluded in conjunction with His Second Coming. According to this view, the future Kingdom of God which is foretold in the Bible and over which Christ is to rule will not be present at any time during the present earth's existence.

The Distinctiveness
Of The Throne Of David

Contrary to one of the Amillennial views, the throne of David cannot be equated with the throne of God in Heaven. Several biblical factors make such an equation incorrect. First, it is a fact of history that several descendants of David have sat upon his throne, but only one descendant of David ever sits on the right hand of God's throne in Heaven. That descendant is Jesus (Ps. 110:1; Heb. 8:1; 12:2; 1 Pet. 3:22).

Second, David's throne was not established until his lifetime. By contrast, since God has always ruled over His creation, His throne in Heaven was established long before David's throne (Ps. 93:1-2).

Third, since God's throne in Heaven was established long before David's throne, and since God's throne certainly was established forever (Lam. 5:19), then it was unnecessary for God to promise to establish David's throne forever (2 Sam. 7:16) if they are the same.

Fourth, in Revelation 3:21 Jesus drew a clear distinction between His throne and the throne of God in Heaven where He presently sits with His Father. Jesus said, "To him that overcometh will I grant to sit with me in my throne, even as I also overcame, and am set down with my Father in his throne." Since it is the throne of David which God has promised to give to Jesus (Lk. 1:31-32), it would appear that David's throne is Jesus' throne. Since Jesus drew a distinction between His throne and God's throne in Heaven, then they must not be the same.

Fifth, God's declaration to His Son, "Thy throne, O God, is forever and ever" (Ps. 45:6-7; Heb. 1:8), seems to indicate that God also recognizes Jesus' throne to be distinct from God's throne in Heaven.

Sixth, it is a fact of history that David's throne was on the earth, not in Heaven. David and his descendants who sat on his throne exercised an earthly ruling authority. Never did they exercise ruling authority in or from Heaven. By contrast, the Bible indicates that God's throne is in Heaven. In fact, it declares that Heaven *is* God's throne. Isaiah 66:1 states, "Thus saith the LORD: The heaven is my throne, and the earth is my footstool" (cf. PS. 103:19; Mt. 5:34; 23:22; Acts 7:49).

These biblical factors force one to conclude that while Jesus sits on the right hand of God's throne in Heaven, He is not sitting on David's throne. This means, then, that Jesus' ministry in Heaven during this present age is not the fulfillment of God's promises concerning David in the Davidic Covenant.

The Future Fulfillment Of The Covenant

Several biblical factors indicate that Christ will fulfill God's promises concerning David in the Davidic Covenant *in the future* (after His Second Coming). First, Daniel 7:13-14 portrayed God's giving the kingdom which lasts forever to the Son of man when that Son comes with the clouds of Heaven. Several things should be noted concerning this portrayal. First, the context of this passage indicated that the Son of man would be given this kingdom after the Roman Empire and its final great ruler (the little horn or Antichrist) have caused terrible tribulation for God's saints and have been judged by God (vv. 11-14, 17-27). Second, it is a fact that Jesus did not come with the clouds of Heaven in His first coming. At that time He came as a humble baby born in a manger. In His Second Coming Jesus will come with the clouds of Heaven. Third, in Matthew 24:29-31 Jesus clearly indicated that He will fulfill the Daniel 7:13-14 prophecy in His Second Coming. Having already referred to the Great Tribulation with the Antichrist (vv. 15-28), Jesus said that immediately after the Tribulation of those days cosmic disturbances will take place in the heavens, "And then shall appear the sign of the Son of man in heaven; and then shall all the tribes of the earth mourn, and they shall see the Son of man coming in the clouds of heaven with power and great glory" (Mt. 24:30). These things indicate that the kingdom over which Christ is to rule was not given to Him in conjunction with His first coming. God will not give it to Him until His Second Coming. Thus, Christ is not exercising that authoritative rule during this present age.

A second factor which denotes a future fulfillment of the Davidic Covenant by Christ is that in Matthew 25:31-46 Jesus declared that He would sit on His throne, judge the Gentiles, and send believers into the kingdom in conjunction with His glorious Second Coming. Thus, He put His throne and kingdom at the Second Coming, not before.

Third, Zechariah 14:4 and 9 disclosed the fact that Messiah will be King after His feet have touched down on the Mount of Olives at His Second Coming.

Fourth, according to Psalm 110:1-2 Messiah is to sit at the right hand of His Father in Heaven *until* it is time for Him to rule. Thus, Messiah's rule as King will not begin until after His present session with the Father in Heaven.

Fifth, Jesus stated that He would sit on the throne of His glory as the Son of man when the earth is regenerated (restored to its prefall condition as the result of the curse of man's sin being lifted from it) [Mt. 19:28; cf. Rom. 8:18-22]. This regeneration of the earth has not happened as yet. When Peter referred to this same change for the earth, he called it "the times of refreshing" and "the times of restitution of all things" (Acts. 3:19-21). Peter made it clear that these times will not come while Jesus is in Heaven. He indicated that they will come when Jesus has returned to be present on earth and when Israel has repented as a nation. The combination of Jesus' and Peter's statements demonstrates that Christ will not sit on His throne until He has returned to earth in His Second Coming.

The Earthly Fulfillment Of The Covenant

Those Amillennialists who believe that Christ fulfills the Davidic Covenant now believe that He does it in His present rule over the Church or over individual human hearts yielded to Him. According to this view, the kingdom over which Christ rules in fulfillment of the Davidic Covenant is solely a *spiritual kingdom*. It is not an earthly kingdom involving rule over everything on planet Earth.

Other Amillennialists who believe that Christ will fulfill the Davidic Covenant in the future believe that He will do it in eternity future after the present earth has been destroyed and history concluded in conjunction with His Second Coming. According to this view, the future Kingdom of God which is foretold in the Bible and over which Christ is to rule will not be present at any time during the present earth's existence.

Although these two Amillennial views disagree with each other on some points, they agree that Christ will never reign over a literal, earthly kingdom on this present earth.

Contrary to this Amillennial agreement, several biblical factors indicate that Christ will fulfill God's promises concerning David in the Davidic Covenant by reigning over a *literal, earthly kingdom on this present earth*. First, according to Zechariah 14:4 and 9, after Messiah's feet have touched down on the Mount of Olives at His Second Coming, He will be King "over all the earth." Christ will rule, not just over the Church or individual human hearts yielded to Him, but over the entire earth (cf. Ps. 72:8; Zech. 9:10; Dan. 2:35, 44-45).

Second, Jeremiah 23:5-8 promised that when Messiah, a righteous Branch of David, reigns as King, He will execute judgment and justice "in the earth." During the days of His rule, the people of Israel will "dwell safely" and will "dwell in their own land." The language of this passage implies an earthly kingdom rule of Christ.

Third, in the Daniel 7 passage observed earlier, the kingdom which God will give to Messiah, the Son of man, when He comes with the clouds of Heaven in His Second Coming (vv. 13-14) is described as "the kingdom and dominion, and the greatness of the kingdom under the whole heaven" (v. 27). The expression *under the whole heaven* indicates that Christ's kingdom will be on the earth (cf. Rev. 11:15).

Fourth, the prophets foretold dramatic changes which are earthly in nature during Messiah's reign. Peter referred to these prophecies in Acts 3:21. Having used the expressions *the times of refreshing* and *the times of restitution of all things* for the period when Christ will be present on the earth after His Second Coming, Peter stated concerning that period, "which God hath spoken by the mouth of all his holy prophets since the age began."

Examples of the dramatic changes foretold by the prophets for Messiah's reign are as follows: Wilderness and desert areas will produce abundantly (Isa. 35:1-2; 41:18-20; 51:3); animals will be completely tame and vegetarian in diet (Isa. 11:6-9; 65:25); diseases and deformities will be healed (Isa. 29:18; 33:24; 35:5-6); longevity of life will be restored (Isa. 65:20-22); a unique stream of water will heal other waters of their problems and will cause great productivity of animal life and abundant fruitage of trees (Ezek. 47:1-12); and food will be plentiful (Isa. 30:23; Ezek. 34:23-29; Joel 2:21-27; 3:18; Amos 9:11-15). Many of these changes which are to be characteristic of Messiah's kingdom rule are very earthly in nature.

Fifth, the chronological order of future events presented in The Book of The Revelation indicates that Christ's kingdom rule is to be *on this present earth* before history is concluded. That order of events is as follows: *first,* the Second Coming of Christ to earth (Rev. 19:11-21); *second,* the imprisonment of Satan in the bottomless pit for 1,000 years (20:1-3); *third,* the kingdom reign of Christ and His saints for 1,000 years (20:4-6); *fourth,* the release of Satan from the bottomless pit after the 1,000 years of Christ's reign are expired (20:7); *fifth,* the revolt of Satan and the unsaved people of the earth against the righteous rule of Christ and His saints, and the divine judgment of that revolt (20:8-9) [several things indicate that this revolt will take place *on the earth* — Satan will deceive the nations located "in the four quarters of the earth"; the rebels will go up "on the breadth of the earth"; and the divine judgment will come "down from God out of heaven"]; *sixth,* the casting of Satan into the lake of fire and brimstone for his eternal judgment (20:10); *seventh,* the appearance of a great white throne and the destruction of the present earth and heaven (20:11); *eighth,* the final judgment of the unsaved and their casting into the lake of fire (20:12-15); and *ninth,* the entrance of eternity future with the appearance of a new heaven and a new earth (21:1). It should be noted that this divinely revealed order of future events portrays the thousand-year reign of Christ taking place on this present earth before it is destroyed, before history is concluded, and before eternity future begins.

Sixth, the Bible presents several characteristics of Messiah's kingdom which will not be true of eternity future. During His reign Messiah will have dominion from sea to sea (Ps. 72:8; Zech. 9:10), but eternity future will have no sea (Rev. 21:1). Unsaved wicked people will be present during Messiah's reign (Isa. 11:4; Rev. 20:8-9), but no such people will be present in the new eternal earth and heaven (Rev. 21:8 — in eternity future all the unsaved will be in the lake of fire). Some people will die during Messiah's reign (Isa. 11:4; Jer. 31:29-30 — rebels will be executed), but there will be no death in eternity future (Rev. 20:14; 21:4). Children will be born during Messiah's reign (Jer. 30:19-20; Ezek. 47:22), but no children will be born in the new eternal earth and heaven. In eternity future all the saints will have immortal bodies which do not marry (Mt. 22:30; 1 Cor. 15:51-53); thus, no children will be born through marriage. In addition, all the saints of eternity future will be sinless, thus no illegitimate children will be born. These contrasts require the conclusion that Christ will reign over a kingdom on this present earth before it is destroyed and before eternity future begins.

The Political Fulfillment Of The Covenant

Amillennialists believe that the kingdom over which Christ is to rule is not political in nature. By contrast, several biblical factors indicate that Christ will fulfill the Davidic Covenant by reigning over *a kingdom which is political in nature*. First, Isaiah 9:6-7 stated that when Messiah sits upon David's throne ruling His kingdom, the government will be upon His shoulder, and the increase of His government will have no end. The term *government* implies literal political rule.

Second, when Messiah reigns He will exercise control over international relations, causing the nations to live together in peace (Isa. 2:4; Mic. 4:3).

Third, during Messiah's reign His capital city, Jerusalem, will be the legal center of the world. Out of it will issue forth the law by which the nations of the world will be governed (Isa. 2:1-3; Mic. 4:1-2).

Fourth, just as David functioned as supreme judge over the affairs of his subjects (2 Sam. 15:2), so Messiah, when He reigns as the Branch of Jesse and David, will function as Supreme Judge over the affairs of His subjects and the nations (Ps. 72:1-4, 12-14; Isa. 2:4; 11:1-5; Jer. 33:14-16; Mic. 4:3). In this function, He will protect the poor, the needy, and the meek of the earth, and He will punish the oppressors and execute the wicked. This is the function of political government (Rom. 13:1-7).

The Certain Fulfillment Of The Covenant

God stated no conditions when He established His covenant with David. Thus, the Davidic Covenant is unconditional in nature. The fulfillment of its promises depends totally upon the faithfulness of God. It is not dependent upon the faithfulness of David or his descendants. This means that the promises are certain to be fulfilled.

The certain fulfillment of the Davidic Covenant is emphasized several times in the Bible. In Psalm 89:28-37 God declared that His covenant with David will stand fast, that He will fulfill its promises in spite of disobedience by David's descendants, that He will not permit His faithfulness to fail. To emphasize this all the more, God said, "My covenant will I not break, nor will I alter the thing that is gone out of my lips. Once have I sworn by my holiness that I will not lie unto David" (vv. 34-35).

Psalm 132:11 asserted that God will not turn back from what He has sworn to David.

After David's descendants had sinned grievously for centuries, God stated that just as humans cannot break the day and night cycle which God has established, so His covenant with David cannot be broken (Jer. 33:20-21). Again He asserted that He will set up a righteous descendant of David to rule as King (Jer. 23:5-6; 33:14-17; Ezek. 37:24-25; Amos 9:11).

Later still God declared His intention to fulfill the promises of the Davidic Covenant in Jesus Christ (Lk. 1:31-33). In all these assertions God stated no conditions and left no doubts concerning the covenant's fulfillment.

Conclusions

In light of the biblical factors examined, it can be concluded that Jesus Christ will fulfill God's promises to David in the Davidic Covenant in the *future* (after His Second Coming to earth). He will do this by establishing and reigning over a *literal, earthly, political kingdom* for 1,000 years *on this present earth*, just as His ancestor David reigned over a literal, earthly, political kingdom on this present earth. If Jesus were to reign over a different kind of kingdom than David did, He would not really be sitting on David's throne exercising David's ruling authority over David's kingdom.

It also can be concluded that this fulfillment is certain to happen and that the Premillennial view agrees with the biblical factors.

TEN

THE NEW COVENANT

The Parties Of The Covenant
According To The Old Testament

A nother significant biblical covenant which will determine important issues related to Israel and the future Kingdom of God is the New Covenant. According to the Old Testament, the parties of this covenant are God and the nation of Israel.

Three things in the Old Testament indicated that God would establish the New Covenant with the people of Israel. First, the Old Testament made clear statements to that effect. For example, Jeremiah 31:31 states, "Behold, the days come, saith the LORD, that I will make a new covenant with the house of Israel, and with the house of Judah." Similar clear statements were made in Isaiah 59:20-21, Jeremiah 50:4-5, Ezekiel 34:25-30, and 37:21-28.

Second, God declared that He would establish the New Covenant with the descendants of those people with whom He established the Mosaic Covenant (the Law). Having promised that He would establish a new covenant with the houses of Israel and Judah, God stated, "Not according to the covenant that I made with their fathers in the day that I took them by the hand to bring them out of the land of Egypt" (Jer. 31:32). Since God gave the Mosaic Law only to the people of Israel (Lev. 26:46; Dt. 4:8) and not to the Gentiles (Rom. 2:14), and since He promised to establish the

New Covenant with the descendants of those to whom He gave the Mosaic Law Covenant, then the New Covenant must also be established with the people of Israel, the physical descendants of Jacob.

Third, the Old Testament associated the establishment of the New Covenant with the endless existence of the nation of Israel (the physical descendants of Jacob) and with the rebuilding and permanent standing of the city of Jerusalem (Jer. 31:31-40).

In light of these three Old Testament factors, it is evident that God intended to establish the New Covenant with the literal people of Israel.

The Promises Of The New Covenant

God promised many things to the people of Israel in the New Covenant. First, He promised regeneration. This would involve the giving of a new heart (a new inner control center where the issues and direction of life are determined) and the new nature (a new favorable spirit or disposition toward God consisting of the law of God written in the heart) [Jer. 31:33; 32:39-40; Ezek. 36:26].

Second, God promised forgiveness of sin (Jer. 31:34; Ezek. 36:25). Third, He pledged the indwelling of the Holy Spirit (Ezek. 36:27). Fourth, He guaranteed a universal knowledge of Jehovah among the people of Israel (Jer. 31:34). The context of this fourth promise indicated that God was referring to a personal experiential knowledge of Himself (the kind of knowledge which comes through a genuine salvation experience), not just a head knowledge of His existence. Fifth, God promised that Israel would obey Him and have a right attitude toward Him forever (Jer. 32:39-40; Ezek. 36:27; 37:23-24).

Sixth, God promised many national blessings to the people of Israel. He pledged that His Spirit and words would never depart from them (Isa. 59:21), that the nation would have a great reputation because of God's special blessing (Isa. 61:8-9), that Israel would have a unique relationship with Him as His special people (Jer. 31:33; Ezek. 36:28), that God would do them good (Jer. 32:40-42), that wild beasts would be eliminated from their land (Ezek. 34:25, 28), that Israel would enjoy complete security in its land (Ezek. 34:25-28), that the nation would receive no more threats and insults from other nations (Ezek. 34:28-29), that great abundance of food would eliminate famine (Ezek. 34:27, 29; 36:29-30), that Israel's land would be so luxurious that it would have the reputation of being like the Garden of Eden (Ezek. 34:29; 36:34-35), that rainfall would be controlled perfectly (Ezek. 34:26), that Israel's cities would be rebuilt and inhabited (Ezek. 36:33), that the nation would enjoy a population explosion (Ezek. 36:37-38; 37:26), that the nation would be completely unified (Ezek. 37:21-22), that the people of Israel would live in their own land forever (Ezek. 37:25), that once again God would have His sanctuary in Israel and would dwell in the midst of the nation forever (Ezek. 37:26-28), and that God would never turn away from the people of Israel (Jer. 32:40).

It should be noted that some of the promises of the New Covenant were purely spiritual in nature, but others were material and national in nature.

The Nature Of The New Covenant

Two things can be said concerning the nature of the New Covenant. First, God intended it to be an *unconditional* covenant. God stated no conditions in the passages which deal with the covenant. This meant that the fulfillment of the promises of the New Covenant would not depend upon the obedience of Israel. In fact, God indicated that He would fulfill the New Covenant's promises, not because Israel would deserve it, but because of Israel's disobedience. In Ezekiel 36:21-22 God declared,

> But I had pity for mine holy name, which the house of Israel had profaned among the nations, to which they went. Therefore, say unto the house of Israel, Thus saith the Lord GOD: I do not this for your sakes, O house of Israel, but for mine holy name's sake, which ye have profaned among the nations, to which ye went (cf. Ezek. 36:32).

In addition, one of the promises of the New Covenant was that God would cause the people of Israel to have a right attitude toward Him and to obey Him (Jer. 32:39-40; Ezek. 36:27; 37:23-24). Thus, instead of the New Covenant being dependent upon Israel's obedience for its fulfillment, it would cause Israel's obedience.

When God presented the promises of the New Covenant, instead of stating conditions for Israel, He continually said, "I will" (Jer. 31:31-34; 32:37-42; Ezek. 36:24-37). This meant that the fulfillment of the promises of the New Covenant would be dependent totally upon God's faithfulness to His Word. God emphasized this fact when He said, "I, the LORD, have spoken it, and I will do it" (Ezek. 36:36).

The second thing which can be said concerning the nature of the New Covenant is that God intended it to be an *everlasting* covenant. He specifically declared it to be everlasting in nature (Isa. 61:8-9; Jer. 32:40; Ezek. 16:60; 37:26). The fact that God intended the New Covenant to be everlasting, together with the fact that it would be unconditional in nature, meant that the New Covenant would never be abolished or annulled with or by Israel. Once it was established, its promises would have to be fulfilled. Once Israel entered into that covenant relationship with God, it would continue in that relationship forever.

The Relationship Of The Church To The New Covenant

As noted earlier, the Old Testament clearly indicated that God would establish the New Covenant with the literal people of Israel, the physical descendants of Jacob. The Old Testament said nothing concerning a relationship of the Church to the New Covenant. This silence should not come as a surprise for at least two reasons. First, the Apostle Paul indicated that no revelation concerning the Church was given before the time of the apostles and New Testament prophets (Eph. 3:2-9). This means that the Old Testament contained no information concerning the Church.

Second, the Old Testament prophets who presented God's revelation concerning the New Covenant were Israelite prophets. It was their responsibility to declare God's message specifically to the people of Israel. Thus, they described how the nation of Israel would be related to the New Covenant, not how others possibly would be related to it. Since the Old Testament contains their declaration of God's message to Israel, one would expect the Old Testament to present only that nation's relationship to the New Covenant.

In spite of the Old Testament's silence concerning the relationship of the Church to the New Covenant, the New Testament seems to indicate that the Church is related somehow to it. There are at least three lines of evidence for this conclusion. First, the Church partakes of the communion service which Jesus instituted on the night before He went to the cross (1. Cor. 10:21; 11:23-30). When Jesus instituted the communion service, He stated the following concerning the cup of that service: "This cup is the new covenant in my blood" (1 Cor. 11:25; Lk. 22:20) [literal translation]. Two things should be noted concerning Jesus' statement. First, since Jesus used the word *the* in the expression *the new covenant,* and since prior to Jesus' statement God had promised only one New Covenant (the one promised to Israel in Jeremiah 31), it seems evident that Jesus was referring to that New Covenant. Thus, Jesus was saying that the cup of the communion service represented the New Covenant which God had promised to literal Israel in Jeremiah 31 and other Old Testament prophetic passages.

Second, Jesus made His statement to Jewish men. The only New Covenant of which they were aware was the one which God had promised to Israel in Jeremiah 31. Since Jesus did not tell them to think otherwise, they understood Him to be referring to that specific New Covenant.

It seems obvious that Jesus was stating that the communion cup represents the New Covenant which God promised to Israel in the Old Testament. The very fact that the Church partakes of the communion cup which represents the New Covenant promised by God to Israel seems to indicate that the Church partakes of that New Covenant.

The second line of evidence for concluding that the Church is related to the New Covenant is that believers who make up the Church partake of the spiritual blessings which God promised as part of the New Covenant in the Old Testament. Church believers have been regenerated (Ti. 3:5), received forgiveness of sin (Eph. 1:7; 4:32; Col. 1:14; 1 Jn. 2:12), been indwelt by the Holy Spirit (1 Cor. 6:19), and received the new nature (a new favorable disposition toward God consisting of the law of God written in the heart) [Rom. 7:22; 2 Cor. 3:3; 2 Pet. 1:4].

The third line of evidence for the Church's relationship to the New Covenant is the Apostle Paul's indication that the apostles of the Church functioned as ministers of a New Covenant (2 Cor. 3:6).

It seems apparent that although the Old Testament promised the New Covenant specifically to the literal nation of Israel, the Church also has a relationship to that covenant. This apparent fact raises an important issue which will now be examined.

The Statement Of The Issue

As previously noted, although the Old Testament promised the New Covenant specifically to the literal nation of Israel, the Church also has a relationship to that covenant. This fact prompts an important question. Since the Church has a relationship to the New Covenant, partaking of its blessings, what is the relationship of the nation of Israel to the fulfillment of that covenant?

Theologians disagree with each other in their answers to this question. Many Covenant Theologians claim that the New Covenant is being fulfilled totally in the Church today. According to this view, the literal nation of Israel forfeited any relationship to the New Covenant because of its unbelief and rebellion against God. The Church in the present age has replaced literal Israel in that relationship. Thus, the promises of the New Covenant which were presented in the Old Testament are to be fulfilled in a spiritualized Israel (the Church) now. They are not to be fulfilled in the literal nation of Israel in the future. Thus, according to this view, there never will be a fulfillment of the New Covenant for national Israel.

By contrast, Dispensational Theologians claim that since God promised to establish the New Covenant with the literal people of Israel (Jer. 31:31), since God intended the New Covenant to be unconditional in nature (totally dependent for the fulfillment of its promises upon God's faithfulness to His Word, Ezek. 36:36), and since God declared that He would fulfill the promises of the New Covenant with Israel, not because the nation would deserve it, but because of its disobedience (Ezek. 36:21-36), then the literal nation of Israel has not forfeited its relationship to the New Covenant because of its unbelief and rebellion against God. According to this view, the Church has not replaced literal Israel in its relationship to the New Covenant, and the New Covenant is not being fulfilled totally in the Church today. In spite of the fact that the Church has a relationship to the New Covenant, that does not rule out the fulfillment of all the promises of the New Covenant with national Israel in the future. Thus, according to the Dispensational view, there will be a fulfillment of the New Covenant for literal Israel in the future.

In light of this disagreement between Covenant and Dispensational Theologians, a conclusion can be drawn. The major issue related to the New Covenant is if there will be a complete fulfillment of the New Covenant with literal, national Israel in the future.

Evidences For The Future Fulfillment Of The New Covenant With National Israel

The Scriptures present several evidences to the effect that God will fulfill the New Covenant with literal, national Israel in the future. First, in one of the major Old Testament passages in which God presented promises of the New Covenant (Ezek. 36:21-38), He clearly indicated that He would fulfill those promises with the same national people who profaned His holy name among the Gentiles. The context (Ezek. 36:16-20) and language ("house of Israel," vv. 22, 32, 37) of this passage make it clear that those people were the literal people of Israel. It is a fact that because of its unbelief, national Israel has not yet received the fulfillment of the New Covenant promises of Ezekiel 36 since the time Jesus established that covenant when He shed His blood on the cross. Since God indicated that He would fulfill the New Covenant promises with literal Israel, and since that nation has not yet received the fulfillment of those promises, one is forced to conclude that they will be fulfilled with national Israel in the future.

Second, God's declaration that He would fulfill the promises of the New Covenant because of Israel's profaning of His holy name among the Gentiles (Ezek. 36:20-23) indicates that literal, national Israel does not forfeit its relationship to the New Covenant. Instead of the nation's disobedience preventing its receiving the fulfillment of the New Covenant promises, it actually causes it.

Third, it was noted earlier that some of the New Covenant promises were purely spiritual in nature, but others were material and national in nature. In addition, it was noted that the Church today partakes of the spiritual blessings which God promised as part of the New Covenant. For example, Church believers experience regeneration and forgiveness of sin, are indwelt by the Holy Spirit, and possess the new nature (the law of God in the heart). The Apostle Paul declared that Church believers have been blessed "with all spiritual blessings" (Eph. 1:3).

It should be noted, however, that although the Church is partaking of the spiritual blessings of the New Covenant, the material and national promises of that covenant are not being fulfilled with the Church. For example, one of the national promises was that once Israel entered into the New Covenant relationship with God, that nation would receive no more threats and insults from other nations (Ezek. 34:28-29). By contrast, in spite of the fact that the Church has had a relationship with the New Covenant throughout its history, it has been threatened, insulted, and persecuted many times by different nations.

Since the material and national promises of the New Covenant are not being fulfilled with the Church, that means that those promises have not yet been fulfilled. Since God has declared His determination to perform all His promises (including the material and national ones) of the New Covenant (Ezek. 36:36), one is forced to conclude that those promises will be fulfilled in the future with the nation of Israel.

Fourth, after the Church came into existence and began to partake of the spiritual blessings of the New Covenant, the Apostle Paul declared that the nation of Israel would experience the fulfillment of the New Covenant when Messiah came in His Second Coming (Rom. 11:25-29). Paul was not original in this declaration, for the Old Testament taught that God would fulfill the New Covenant with Israel when Messiah came in conjunction with Israel's final regathering from its dispersion and permanent restoration to the land of Israel (Is. 59:20-21; Jer. 32:37-44; 50:4-5; Ezek. 36:22-28; 37:21-28).

Paul stated that God would not repent (change His mind) concerning this future calling for Israel which He announced in the Old Testament (Rom. 11:29). In other words, God's calling for Israel to enter into New Covenant relationship with Him in the future is irrevocable. It must happen. Paul indicated that when Israel enters into that relationship with God, the Isaiah 59:20-21 New Covenant prophecy will be fulfilled.

The fact that Paul had literal, national Israel in mind when he made these statements in Romans 11 is evident from at least three things. First, in verse one he clearly indicated that he was talking about the people of God who were as much literal Israelites, physical descendants of Abraham, and members of Israelite tribes as he was. Second, in verse 14 Paul declared that the Israel to which he referred was his flesh (that is, his own countrymen). Third, Paul contrasted the Israel of this chapter with the Gentiles (vv. 11-14, 25).

It is evident that in Romans 11 Paul was teaching that literal, national Israel will enter into New Covenant relationship with God in conjunction with the Second Coming of Messiah.

The fact that Paul taught this *after* the Church had come into existence and had begun to partake of the spiritual blessings of the New Covenant indicates two things. First, it indicates that the literal nation of Israel has not forfeited its promised relationship to the New Covenant because of its unbelief and rebellion against God. Second, it indicates that although the Church is partaking of the spiritual blessings of the New Covenant, it has not replaced literal Israel in its promised relationship to the New Covenant. In line with this, Paul clearly stated that God has not cast away His people of Israel (Rom. 11:1-2).

Concluding Considerations

It is apparent that Jesus established the New Covenant when He shed His blood on the cross (Lk. 22:20; 1 Cor. 11:25; Heb. 8:6-13; 9:15; 12:24). The Church, which began shortly after Christ's death (Acts 2:1-4; 11:15), has partaken of the spiritual blessings of the New Covenant. According to the Apostle Paul's teaching in Romans 11, during the time of the Church, a remnant of literal, national Israel is being saved by the grace of God through faith in Christ. Those Israelites who make up that remnant become members of the Church through salvation. They thereby partake of the spiritual blessings of the New Covenant, as do the other members of the Church. They do not, however, partake of the material and national blessings of the New Covenant, as the rest of the Church does not.

By contrast with the remnant, during the time of the Church, the majority of literal, national Israel does not become saved because of its hardened unbelief. As a result, that majority does not obtain any of the promised blessings of the New Covenant, even though it seeks many of those blessings during the present Church age. Because of their unbelief, the Israelites who make up the majority of the nation have been removed by God from the place of covenant blessing which the nation of Israel enjoyed with God in the past. This means, then, that national Israel failed to enter the New Covenant relationship with God in conjunction with Messiah's first coming.

While the majority of national Israel remains in unbelief outside the place of covenant blessing, many Gentiles, who originally were not in that place of blessing, are being grafted into it by the grace of God through faith in Christ. These saved Gentiles are members of the Church. They are grafted into the place of covenant blessing in the sense that they partake of the spiritual blessings of the New Covenant, as do the remnant Israelite members of the Church.

In spite of the fact that believing Gentiles are grafted into the place of covenant blessing in place of the unbelieving majority of national Israel, that does not mean that the fulfillment of the New Covenant with literal, national Israel has been nullified. Paul made it very clear that the majority of national Israel will not be removed from the place of covenant blessing forever. That removal is only temporary. When the great harvest of Gentile souls has been gathered and Messiah returns, national Israel will be saved and placed back into the place of covenant blessing (Rom. 11:23-27). As a result, at that time literal, national Israel will enter fully into the New Covenant relationship with God, and all the promises (spiritual, material, and national) of that covenant will be fulfilled completely with that nation. Thus, although national Israel failed to enter the New Covenant relationship with God in conjunction with Messiah's first coming, it will enter that relationship in conjunction with His Second Coming.

In Romans 11, therefore, Paul explained how the Church now partakes of the spiritual blessings of the New Covenant. The complete fulfillment of that covenant with national Israel, however, has not been and never will be nullified.

ELEVEN

A DESCRIPTION
AND EARLY HISTORY OF
MILLENNIAL VIEWS

D uring the history of the Church, three major views have been held concerning the future Kingdom of God foretold in such passages as Daniel 2 and 7. Today those three views are called Premillennialism, Amillennialism, and Postmillennialism. The names of these views all contain the term *millennialism* (a form of the word *millennium*). They are using this common form as a synonym or substitute for the expression *the Kingdom of God.*

Premillennialism

The prefix *pre* means *before.* Thus, Premillennialism is the view which states that Christ will return to earth *before* the Millennium or Kingdom of God. Christ will return in His Second Coming for the purpose of establishing the Kingdom of God on earth. This kingdom will last for 1,000 years on this present earth (Rev. 20:1-7), and it will be a literal, political kingdom with Christ ruling worldwide as King together with the saints of God.

The word *millennium* was derived from the concept of 1,000 years. It is the combination of two Latin words: *mille* (1,000) and *annum* (year). In the early days of the Church, the premillennial view was called *chiliasm* (derived from the Greek word meaning 1,000).

Amillennialism

The prefix *a* means *no*. Thus, Amillennialism is the view which states that there will be *no* literal, political Kingdom of God on this earth. The future Kingdom of God foretold in such passages as Daniel 2 and 7 is totally spiritual in nature. It consists either of the Church of this age or of Christ's present rule from Heaven over the hearts of believing human beings or the future eternal state. When Christ returns to earth in His Second Coming, there will be a general resurrection of all the dead, a general judgment, the end of this present earth, and the immediate beginning of the future eternal state.

Postmillennialism

The prefix *post* means *after*. Thus, Postmillennialism is the view which states that Christ will return to this earth *after* the Millennium or Kingdom of God. There will be a literal Kingdom of God on this earth, but it will not be established through the supernatural intervention of Christ into history at His Second Coming. Instead, it will be established through human efforts, such as man's expanding knowledge, his new discoveries and inventions, his increasing ability to exercise dominion over nature, and the expanding influence of the Church. The Church has the responsibility to help bring in the Kingdom. Christ's Second Coming will occur at the close of the Millennium as the crowning event of that golden age.

The History Of The Millennial Views

During the history of the Church, views of the Millennium have gone through four stages of development. These will be examined in the chronological order of their appearance.

Early Premillennialism

Numerous historians declare that Premillennialism (initially called chiliasm) was the first major millennial view of the Church and that it was the predominant view of orthodox believers from the first to the third centuries. A sampling of historians will be quoted as evidence for this declaration.

Edward Gibbon (1737-1794), the noted English historian who wrote the classic work *The History of the Decline and Fall of the Roman Empire,* stated the following:

> The ancient and popular doctrine of the Millennium was intimately connected with the second coming of Christ. As the works of the creation had been finished in six days, their duration in their present state, according to a tradition which was attributed to the prophet Elijah, was fixed to six thousand years. By the same analogy it was inferred, that this long period of labor and contention, which was now almost elapsed, would be succeeded by a joyful Sabbath of a thousand years; and that Christ, with the triumphant band of the saints and the elect who had escaped death, or who had been miraculously revived, would reign upon earth till the time appointed for the last and general resurrection.
>
> ·
>
> The assurance of such a Millennium was carefully inculcated by a succession of fathers from Justin Martyr and Irenaeus, who conversed with the immediate disciples of the apostle, down to Lactantius, who was preceptor to the son of Constantine. Though it might not be universally received, it appears to have been the reigning sentiment of the orthodox believers.[1]

It should be noted that Gibbon had an unfriendly attitude toward Christianity; therefore, he was not biased in favor of Premillennialism. His comments have added significance in light of that fact.

J. C. I. Gieseler, Professor of Theology at the university in Gottingen, Germany, in the early 19th century, a highly acclaimed Church historian in his time and himself not a premillennialist, wrote the following when referring to some early Christian literature which was produced between 117 and 193 A.D.: "In all these works the belief in the Millennium is so evident, that no one can hesitate to consider it as universal in an age, when certainly such motives as it offered were not unnecessary to animate men to suffer for Christianity."[2]

Henry C. Sheldon, Professor of Historical Theology at Boston University in the late 19th century, said that chiliasm "was entertained in the second century not only by Ebionites, and by writers who, like Cerinthus, mixed with their Gnosticism a large element of Judaism, but by many (very likely a majority) of those in the Catholic Church."[3] It should be noted that Sheldon used the term *Catholic* (which means *universal*) to refer to the entire organized Church. This was the sense of that term during the early centuries before the Roman Catholic system was formed.

Philip Schaff, prominent German Reformed theologian and Church historian in America during the major part of the 19th century, stated the following concerning the early Church (100-325 A.D.) in his monumental eight-volume *History of the Christian Church*:

> The most striking point in the eschatology of the ante-Nicene age is the prominent chiliasm, or millennarianism, that is the belief of a visible reign of Christ in glory on earth with the risen saints for a thousand years, before the general resurrection and judgment. It was indeed not the doctrine of the

church embodied in any creed or form of devotion, but a widely current opinion of distinguished teachers, such as Barnabas, Papias, Justin Martyr, Irenaeus, Tertullian, Methodius, and Lactantius.[4]

Adolph Harnack, Lutheran theologian and Church historian in Germany during the late 19th and early 20th centuries and recognized authority on Ante-Nicene Church history (100-325 A.D.), wrote the following:

> First in point of time came the faith in the nearness of Christ's second advent and the establishing of His reign of glory on the earth. Indeed it appears so early that it might be questioned whether it ought not to be regarded as an essential part of the Christian religion.[5]
>
> ·
>
> ...it must be admitted that this expectation was a prominent feature in the earliest proclamation of the gospel, and materially contributed to its success. If the primitive churches had been under the necessity of framing a "Confession of Faith," it would certainly have embraced those pictures by means of which the near future was distinctly realized.[6]

Harnack also stated that "In the anticipations of the future prevalent amongst the early Christians (c. 50-150) it is necessary to distinguish a fixed...element." He indicated that the following items were included in that fixed element: "(1) the notion that a last terrible battle with the enemies of God was impending; (2) the faith in the speedy return of Christ; (3) the conviction that Christ will judge all men, and (4) will set up a kingdom of glory on earth."[7]

Harnack declared that among other early Christian beliefs concerning the future "was the expectation that the future Kingdom of Christ on earth should have a fixed duration,

— according to the most prevalent opinion, a duration of one thousand years. From this fact the whole ancient Christian eschatology was known in later times as 'chiliasm.' "[8]

Harnack claimed that in their eschatology the early Christians preserved the Jewish hopes for the future presented in ancient Jewish literature.[9]

He also asserted that Justin Martyr, a prominent early Christian writer (100-165 A.D.) who had been saved out of pagan Greek philosophy, "speaks of chiliasm as a necessary part of complete orthodoxy, although he knows Christians who do not accept it."[10] Harnack made this significant observation: "That a philosopher like Justin, with a bias towards an Hellenic construction of the Christian religion, should nevertheless have accepted its chiliastic elements is the strongest proof that these enthusiastic expectations were inseparably bound up with the Christian faith down to the middle of the 2nd century."[11]

It should be noted that Harnack was strongly liberal in his theology; therefore, he was not biased in favor of Premillennialism. In light of this fact, his comments take on added significance.

Will Durant, the 20th-century historian who produced the multi-volume set entitled *The Story of Civilization*, wrote the following concerning Jesus Christ's view of the Kingdom of God:

> What did he mean by the Kingdom? A supernatural heaven? Apparently not, for the apostles and the early Christians unanimously expected an earthly Kingdom. This was the Jewish tradition that Christ inherited; and he taught his followers to pray to the Father, "Thy Kingdom come, thy will be done on earth as it is in heaven."[12]

Durant further declared that "The apostles were apparently unanimous in believing that Christ would soon return to establish the Kingdom of Heaven on earth."[13] Then he stated that "One faith united the scattered congregations: that Christ was the son of God, that he would return to establish his Kingdom on earth, and that all who believed in him would at the Last Judgment be rewarded with eternal bliss."[14]

Just a few historians have been quoted who have claimed that Premillennialism was the first and predominant millennial view of the Church. If space permitted, many others who have made the same claim could be cited. Research indicates that numerous such historians were not premillennialists themselves. In fact, many were opposed to the premillennial view personally. The fact that scholars who were not biased in favor of Premillennialism would assert that it was the first and predominant millennial·view of the Church is quite significant. It indicates that they based their assertion upon evidence which they were convinced was too strong to be denied.

Much of the evidence which these historians use to substantiate their claim is found in the writings of early Church leaders. Some of these writings will now be examined.

The Millennial View of Early Church Leaders

Papias

Papias lived from approximately 60 to 130 A.D. It is believed that he was taught directly by the Apostle John. He was a friend of Polycarp, another prominent Church leader who was a disciple of John. Papias served as Bishop of Hierapolis in Phrygia, Asia Minor. His writings have not been preserved to the present day; however, Irenaeus and Eusebius, two other Church leaders, referred to his writings.[15]

Irenaeus, after relating Christ's teaching concerning the dramatic changes which the earth will experience in the future Millennium, wrote, "And these things are borne witness to in writing by Papias, the hearer of John, and a companion of Polycarp, in his fourth book.[16]

Eusebius, Bishop of Caesarea and the "Father of Church history,"[17] wrote concerning Papias in his work *Ecclesiastical History* (III, 39), "Among other things he says that a thousand years will elapse after the resurrection of the dead and there will be a corporal establishment of Christ's Kingdom on this earth."[18]

The Epistle of Barnabas

Scholars have concluded that this piece of early Christian literature was written between 120 and 150 A.D. by a Christian in Alexandria, Egypt, not by the Barnabas of the New Testament.[19]

This epistle presented a view which appears to have been rather popular among ancient Jews and Christians. It declared that just as God labored for six days in creation, so the present earth will labor in its turmoil for 6,000 years. Then it asserted that just as God rested on the seventh day after His six days of labor, so the present earth will enjoy 1,000 years of rest after its 6,000 years of labor. This thousand years of rest will begin "When His Son, coming [again], shall destroy the time of the wicked man, and judge the ungodly, and change the sun, and the moon, and the stars."[20] In other words, the thousand years of rest will begin in conjunction with the Second Coming of Christ.

The epistle further stated that after the earth's seventh day (thousand years of rest), there will be an "eighth day, that is, a beginning of another world."[21] It would appear that this "eighth day" is a reference to the future eternal state with the new eternal earth after the thousand-year Millennium.

Justin Martyr

Justin Martyr lived from approximately 100 to 165 A.D. He was well-educated. He held no regular church office but served as a traveling evangelist and defender of Christianity. In his writings he argued for the superiority of Christianity to paganism and Judaism. On his second journey to Rome he was arrested, lashed, and beheaded because of his testimony for Christ.[22]

In his writing entitled *Dialogue With Trypho* Justin stated, "But I and others, who are right-minded Christians on all points, are assured that there will be a resurrection of the dead, and a thousand years in Jerusalem, which will then be built, adorned, and enlarged, [as] the prophets Ezekiel and Isaiah and others declare."[23] His use of the expression *right-minded Christians on all points* was his way of asserting that Premillennialism was the orthodox view in his day.

Again Justin said,

> And further, there was a certain man with us, whose name was John, one of the apostles of Christ, who prophesied, by a revelation that was made to him, that those who believed in our Christ would dwell a thousand years in Jerusalem; and that thereafter the general, and, in short, the eternal resurrection and judgment of all men would likewise take place.[24]

In this statement Justin referred to John's declarations in Revelation 20. In that passage John asserted that Christ and His saints will reign for 1,000 years. Justin's statement indicates that he understood John to be referring to 1,000 *literal* years.

Irenaeus

Irenaeus received his early Christian training from Polycarp, Bishop of Symrna in western Asia Minor. Polycarp had been a disciple of the Apostle John. Irenaeus may have served under Polycarp for several years before being sent to Gaul (France) as a missionary. Around 178 A.D. Irenaeus became Bishop of Lyons in Gaul. There he continued to serve effectively during the last quarter of the second century.[25]

Irenaeus wrote the following concerning the blessings of the future Kingdom of God foretold in the Scriptures:

The predicted blessing, therefore, belongs unquestionably to the times of the kingdom, when the righteous shall bear rule upon their rising from the dead; when also the creation, having been renovated and set free, shall fructify with an abundance of all kinds of food, from the dew of heaven, and from the fertility of the earth: as the elders who saw John, the disciple of the Lord, related that they had heard from him how the Lord used to teach in regard to these times.[26]

Irenaeus declared that in conjunction with the future Kingdom and its renovation of nature, the Lord promised great fruitage of vines, abundance of grain, large productivity of fruit-bearing trees, seeds and grass, "and that all animals feeding [only] on the productions of the earth, should [in those days] become peaceful and harmonious among each other, and be in perfect subjection to man."[27]

According to Irenaeus, in Isaiah 11:6-9 Isaiah prophesied concerning this future time when all animals will be tame and vegetarian in diet as they were before the fall of man. Commenting on this prophecy, he said, "And it is right that when the creation is restored, all the animals should obey and be in subjection to man, and revert to the food originally given by God (for they had been originally subjected in obedience to Adam), that is, the productions of the earth."[28]

Irenaeus warned against any attempts to allegorize the Kingdom prophecies: "If, however, any shall endeavor to allegorize [prophecies] of this kind, they shall not be found consistent with themselves in all points and shall be confuted by the teaching of the very expression [in question]."[29]

With regard to prophecies concerning the resurrection of saints, Irenaeus wrote:

For all these and other words were unquestionably
spoken in reference to the resurrection of the just,
which takes place after the coming of Antichrist,
and the destruction of all nations under his rule;
in [the times of] which [resurrection] the righteous
shall reign in the earth, waxing stronger by the
sight of the Lord; and through Him they shall
become accustomed to partake in the glory of God
the Father, and shall enjoy in the kingdom
intercourse and communion with the holy angels.[30]

Along the same lines he said the following concerning
John's comments in Revelation 20: "John, therefore, did
distinctly foresee the first 'resurrection of the just,' and the
inheritance in the kingdom of the earth; and what the
prophets have prophesied concerning it harmonize [with
his vision]."[31]

These statements indicate that Irenaeus was convinced
that saints will be resurrected from the dead to reign with
Christ in His Kingdom on this earth. Concerning conditions
on the earth during the Kingdom he said, "But in the times
of the kingdom, the earth has been called again by Christ
[to its pristine condition], and Jerusalem rebuilt after the
pattern of the Jerusalem above."[32]

Irenaeus stated that after the times of the Kingdom, the
great white throne will appear, the present heavens and
earth will flee away, the unjust will be resurrected and
judged, the new heaven and earth will come into existence,
and the new Jerusalem will descend from heaven to earth.[33]

Tertullian

Tertullian lived from approximately 160 to 220 A.D. He
was thoroughly trained for politics, the practice of law, and
public debate. After he was converted around 195 A.D. he
devoted his life to the defense of Christianity against

paganism, Judaism, and heresy. He opposed infant baptism, promoted the Traducian theory of the origin of the human soul, and developed the term *trinity* to describe the Godhead. In the later years of his life he became associated with Montanism, a movement which some regarded to be a heretical sect.[34]

In a work which he wrote before his association with Montanism, Tertullian stated, "But we do confess that a kingdom is promised to us upon the earth, although before heaven, only in another state of existence; inasmuch as it will be after the resurrection for a thousand years."[35]

Then he wrote, "After its thousand years are over,...there will ensue the destruction of the world and the conflagration of all things at the judgments."[36]

Lactantius

Lactantius lived from approximately 240 to 320 A.D. He was trained in rhetoric (the effective use of language in literature and oratory).[37] By 290 A.D. he had been appointed by Emperor Diocletian to teach rhetoric at a school in Nicomedia. He became a Christian around 300 A.D. and suffered greatly under the persecution by Emperor Galerius. After Emperor Constantine granted freedom to the Church and declared himself a Christian, he appointed Lactantius to be the personal teacher of his son.[38] Through his writings in defense of Christianity he became known as "the Christian Cicero."[39] Jerome designated him the most learned man of his time.[40] Eusebius and Augustine honored him.[41]

Lactantius wrote,

> And as God labored six days in building such great works, so His religion and the truth must labor during these six thousand years, while malice prevails and dominates. And again, since He rested on the seventh day from His completed labors and blessed that day, so it is necessary that, at the end

of the six thousandth year, all evil be abolished from the earth, and that justice reign for a thousand years, and that there be tranquility and rest from the labors which the world is now enduring for so long.[42]

Lactantius understood that the end of this present age will be characterized by a time of unprecedented tribulation:

As the end of this age is drawing near, therefore, it is necessary that the state of human affairs be changed and fall to a worse one, evil growing stronger, so that these present times of ours, in which iniquity and malice have advanced to a very high peak, can be judged, however, happy and almost golden in comparison with that irremediable evil.[43]

He followed this statement with an amazing description of the future Tribulation period.[44]

Although he lived while Rome was the great world power, Lactantius was convinced from the prophetic Scriptures that Rome would be destroyed and that then the rule of the world would shift from the west to the east: "This will be the cause of the destruction and confusion, that the Roman name, by which the world is now ruled — the mind shudders to say it, but I will say it, because it is going to be — will be taken from the earth, and power will be returned to Asia, and again the Orient will dominate and the West will serve."[45]

Lactantius believed that at His Second Coming Christ will war against and judge Antichrist and his godless forces.[46] Then "the dead will rise again,...so that they may reign with God for a thousand years after being again restored to life."[47]

He said of Jesus, "When He shall have destroyed injustice and made the great judgment and restored to life those who were just from the beginning, He will stay among men for a thousand years and will rule them with just dominion."[48]

125

Lactantius described conditions of the future Kingdom:
Then, those who will be living in bodies will not die, but will generate an infinite multitude during those same thousand years,...Those who will be raised from the dead will be in charge of the living as judges.[49]

At this same time, also, the prince of demons who is the contriver of all evils will be bound in chains, and he will be in custody for the thousand years of the heavenly power whereby justice will reign on earth, lest any evil be exerted against the people of God...the holy city will be set up in the center of the earth in which the Founder Himself may abide with the just who are its rulers.[50]

Lactantius claimed that the earth will be transformed; the sun will be more effective; fertility will be great; crops will be abundant, and animals will be tame.[51] In light of these changes he said:

Men will enjoy, therefore, the most tranquil and most abundant life, and they will reign together with God. Kings of the nations will come from the ends of the earth with gifts and presents to adore and honor the great King, whose name will be famous and venerable to all peoples which will be under heaven and to the kings who will rule on the earth.[52]

Lactantius asserted that at the end of the thousand years Satan will be set loose to lead a final revolt. God will crush the revolt and judge Satan forever. The unjust will be resurrected to everlasting sufferings. Heaven and earth will change drastically.[53]

This examination of early Church leaders indicates that they were, indeed, Premillennial by conviction.

THE REJECTION OF PREMILLENNIALISM AND DEVELOPMENT OF AMILLENNIALISM AND POSTMILLENNIALISM

The Rejection of Premillennialism in the East

Although Premillennialism was the predominant view of orthodox Christians from the first to the third centuries, eventually it was superseded by a new millennial view — Amillennialism (also called allegorical Millennialism by some).[1] By the fifth century Amillennialism had been developed to replace early Premillennialism.

The rejection of Premillennialism began with some leaders of the Greek Church in the east during the second century. As early as 170 A.D. a church group (known as the Alogi) in Asia Minor rejected the prophetic writings from which the premillennial view was derived. This group "denounced the Apocalypse of John as a book of fables."[2]

Several factors contributed to this rejection of the premillennial view in the east. First was the Montanistic controversy which raged around 160 to 220 A.D.[3] The Montanists were a church group who, because of certain beliefs which they emphasized, became controversial. Christians who did not share their views came to regard them as extremists and even heretics. Because the Montanists were also premillennial by conviction, and because some carried their Premillennialism to extremes not supported by the Scriptures, some leaders of the Greek Church became suspicious of the entire premillennial view. They began to associate Premillennialism with extremism and heresy since it was advocated strongly by an extremist, heretical group. Premillennialism began to be discredited through guilt by association.

Second, some Church leaders feared the teaching of Premillennialism that Christ at His Second Coming would crush the Roman power and take over the rule of the world. They were afraid that this teaching would be "a source of political danger," that it would bring greater persecution against the Church from the Roman Empire.[4] To their way of thinking, it was expedient to sacrifice the premillennial view in order to avoid more intense persecution.

Third, some churches were convinced that the premillennial emphasis upon the glorious Kingdom reign of Christ in the future drew attention away from the organizational structure and programs which they had developed. As a result, they feared that Premillennialism posed a threat to the very existence and function of the Church in the present.[5]

Fourth, there was a strong anti-Semitic spirit in the eastern church. Because the majority of Jews of Jesus' day had rejected Him, and since so many of their successors refused to believe in Him, Gentiles who professed to be Christians increasingly called Jews "Christ-killers" and developed a strong bias against anything Jewish. Because the premillennial belief in the earthly, political Kingdom rule of Messiah in the future was the same hope which had motivated the Jews for centuries, that belief was increasingly "stigmatized as 'Jewish' and consequently 'heretical' " by eastern Gentile Christians.[6] Once again Premillennialism was discredited through guilt by association.

Fifth, a new theology, known as Alexandrian theology, developed in the Greek Church.[7] This new theology was formed by Origen (185-253 A.D.) and other Church scholars in Alexandria, Egypt. Because of his brilliance, Origen was appointed president of the important theology school of

Alexandria when only 18 years of age.[8] As a result of that position and his exceptional abilities, he had extensive influence.

Origen and his associates were intensely interested in pagan Greek philosophy. They examined it extensively. Origen studied under "the heathen Ammonius Saccas, the celebrated founder of Neo-Platonism."[9] He and other Alexandrian Church scholars tried to integrate Greek philosophy with Christian doctrine. This attempted integration played a significant role in the development of the new Alexandrian theology.

Much of Greek philosophy advocated that anything which is physical or material is inherently evil, and only the totally spiritual or nonphysical is good. Through this influence the Alexandrian scholars developed the idea that an earthly, political Kingdom with physical blessings would be an evil thing, and that only a totally spiritual, nonphysical Kingdom would be good. That idea prompted Alexandrian theology to reject the premillennial belief in an earthly, political Kingdom of God with physical blessings.

One historian expressed this transition as follows:

> The influence of Greek thought upon Christian theology undermined the millennarian world view in another, possibly more significant, manner. In the theology of the great 3rd-century Alexandrian Christian thinker Origen, the focus was not upon the manifestation of the kingdom within this world but within the soul of the believer, a significant shift of interest away from the historical toward the metaphysical, or the spiritual.[10]

Because of the great influence of the Alexandrian scholars, most of the Greek Church followed their lead in rejecting Premillennialism. Concerning this rejection of the premillennial views in the east, Harnack wrote, "It was the Alexandrian theology that superseded them; that is to say, Neo-Platonic mysticism triumphed over the early Christian hope of the future."[11] Again he stated that "mysticism" played a significant role in giving "the death-blow to chiliasm in the Greek Church."[12]

Sixth, Origen developed a new method of interpreting the Bible. This method has been called the allegorical or spiritualizing method, and it stands in contrast to the literal, historical-grammatical method. This permitted him to read almost any meaning he desired into the Bible, and it led him into heresy in certain areas of doctrine (for example, he rejected the idea of physical resurrection and believed in universal salvation for all human beings and fallen angels).[13] Concerning this approach by Origen to the interpretation of the Scriptures, Schaff has written,

His great defect is the neglect of the grammatical and historical sense and his constant desire to find a hidden mystic meaning. He even goes further in this direction than the Gnostics, who everywhere saw transcendental, unfathomable mysteries...His allegorical interpretation is ingenious, but often runs far away from the text and degenerates into the merest caprice.[14]

Premillennialism is strongly based upon the literal, historical-grammatical interpretation of those Old Testament passages which the prophets wrote concerning the future Kingdom of God. In his opposition to Premillennialism, Origen spiritualized the language of the prophets.[15] Once again, because of Origen's great influence, this allegorical method of interpreting the prophets was widely accepted by the Greek Church.

Seventh, the Greek Church rejected the Book of Revelation from the canon of Scripture. Around 260 A.D. Nepos, an

Egyptian Church bishop, tried "to overthrow the Origenistic Theology and vindicate chiliasm by exegetical methods."[16] Although several churches supported his endeavor, Nepos' efforts eventually were defeated by Dionysius, who had been trained by Origen. Dionysius succeeded in "asserting the allegorical interpretation of the prophets as the only legitimate exegesis."[17]

Harnack related the following information concerning the controversy between Dionysius and Nepos:

> During this controversy Dionysius became convinced that the victory of mystical theology over "Jewish" chiliasm would never be secure so long as the Apocalypse of John passed for an apostolic writing and kept its place among the homologoumena of the canon. He accordingly raised the question of the apostolic origin of the Apocalypse; and by reviving old difficulties, with ingenious arguments of his own, he carried his point.[18]

Dionysius so prejudiced the Greek Church against the Book of Revelation and its canonicity that during the fourth century that church removed it from its canon of Scripture, "and thus the troublesome foundation on which chiliasm might have continued to build was got rid of."[19] The Greek Church kept the Book of Revelation out of its canon for several centuries, "and consequently chiliasm remained in its grave."[20] The Greek Church restored the book to its canon late in the Middle Ages, but by that time the damage to the premillennial view could not be remedied.[21]

It should be noted that although the Greek Church rejected Premillennialism, other church groups in the east, such as the Armenian Church and the Semitic churches of Syria, Arabia, and Ethiopia, held on to Premillennialism for a considerably longer time.[22]

The Rejection Of Premillennialism In The West

The Western or Latin Church remained strongly premillennial longer than the Greek Church in the east. Harnack stated that "in the west millennarianism was still a point of 'orthodoxy' in the 4th century."[23] The reason for the longer duration of premillennial belief in the west was twofold. First, through the fourth century many western theologians "escaped the influence of Greek speculation."[24] Second, the western church always recognized the apostolic authorship and canonicity of the Book of Revelation.[25]

A change began to develop, however. After the fourth century the western church started to join the revolt against premillennial belief. Two major factors contributed to this change. First, Alexandrian theology was brought to the west by such influential church leaders as Jerome and Ambrose. As a result of being taught by Greek theologians in the east for several years, Jerome (345-420 A.D.) declared that he had been delivered from "Jewish opinions," and he ridiculed the early premillennial beliefs.[26] Concerning those early beliefs, Harnack declared that Jerome "and the other disciples of the Greeks did a great deal to rob them of their vitality."[27]

The second major factor which prompted the rejection of Premillennialism in the west was the teaching of Augustine (354-430 A.D.), the Bishop of Hippo, concerning the Church. Augustine himself had been a premillennialist in the early days of his Christian faith; however, through time he rejected that view in favor of a new one which he developed.[28] That new view became known as Amillennialism.

Several things prompted this change in Augustine. First, the political situation of the Church had changed radically around the period of his life. By Augustine's time the persecution of the Church by Rome had stopped, and the state had made itself the servant of the Church. As the Roman

Empire crumbled, the Church stood fast, ready to rule in place of the empire. It looked as if Gentile world dominion was being crushed and that the Church was becoming victorious over it.[29]

Under these circumstances Augustine concluded that Premillennialism was obsolete, that it did not fit the changed situation. In place of it he developed the idea that the Church is the Kingdom of Messiah foretold in such Scriptures as Daniel 2 and 7 and Revelation 20. In his book, *The City of God*, he became the first person to teach the idea that the organized Catholic (universal) Church is the Messianic Kingdom and that the Millennium began with the first coming of Christ.[30] Augustine wrote, "The saints reign with Christ during the same thousand years, understood in the same way, that is, of the time of His first coming,"[31] and, "Therefore the Church even now is the kingdom of Christ, and the kingdom of heaven. Accordingly, even now His saints reign with Him."[32]

The second factor which prompted Augustine to reject Premillennialism was his negative reaction to his own pleasure-seeking, self-indulgent, immoral lifestyle in his preconversion days. "After his conversion to Christianity, Augustine, a former *bon vivant*, consistently favoured a world-denying and ascetic style of life."[33] This led him to reject "as carnal any expectations of a renewed and purified world that the believers could expect to enjoy."[34]

The third factor in his change of view was the influence of Greek philosophy upon his thinking. Before his conversion Augustine was deeply immersed in the study of this philosophy, much of which asserted the inherent evil of the physical or material and the inherent goodness of the totally spiritual. This philosophy continued to leave its mark upon him even after his conversion. It also prompted him to reject as carnal the premillennial idea of an earthly, political

Kingdom of God with great material blessings. To his way of thinking, in order for the Kingdom of God to be good, it must be spiritual in nature. Thus, "for him the millennium had become a spiritual state into which the Church collectively had entered at Pentecost...and which the individual Christian might already enjoy through mystical communion with God."[35]

Concerning the premillennial opinion Augustine wrote,

> And this opinion would not be objectionable, if it were believed that the joys of the saints in that Sabbath shall be spiritual, and consequent on the presence of God; for I myself, too, once held this opinion. But, as they assert that those who then rise again shall enjoy the leisure of immoderate carnal banquets, furnished with an amount of meat and drink such as not only to shock the feeling of the temperate, but even to surpass the measure of credulity itself, such assertions can be believed only by the carnal. They who do believe them are called by the spiritual Chiliasts, which we may literally reproduce by the name Millenarians.[36]

In order to avoid the implications of some of the millennial passages in the Bible, Augustine applied Origen's allegorical method of interpretation to the prophets and the Book of Revelation. For example, according to Augustine the abyss in which Satan is confined during the millennial reign of Christ (Rev. 20:1-3) is not a literal location or place. Instead, he said, "By the *abyss* is meant the countless multitude of the wicked whose hearts are unfathomably deep in malignity against the Church of God."[37] His interpretation of Satan's being cast into the abyss was as follows: "He is said to be cast in thither, because, when prevented from harming believers, he takes more complete possession of the ungodly."[38] He said that the binding and shutting up of Satan in the abyss "means his being more unable to seduce the Church."[39] Augustine was convinced that this binding of Satan in the abyss is a reality during this present Church age.[40]

In addition, Augustine interpreted the first resurrection (referred to by John in conjunction with the establishment of the millennial reign of Christ, Rev. 20:4-6) as being not the future bodily resurrection of believers but the present spiritual resurrection of the soul which takes place at the new birth.[41]

"Augustine's allegorical millennialism became the official doctrine of the church," and Premillennialism went underground.[42] Some aspects of Premillennialism were even branded as heretical.[43] The Roman Catholic Church strongly advocated and maintained Augustine's amillennial view throughout the Middle Ages. During that span of time occasional premillennial groups formed to challenge the doctrine and political power of the major part of organized Christendom, but they were not able to restore Premillennialism to its original position as the accepted, orthodox view of the Church. Many Anabaptists were premillennial by conviction during the Reformation era. Some of these were quite radical in their Premillennialism, but many were not.[44] The Lutheran, Reformed, and Anglican reformers rejected Premillennialism as being "Jewish opinions."[45] They maintained the amillennial view which the Roman Catholic Church had adopted from Augustine.[46]

The Revolt Against Amillennialism

Augustine's Amillennialism remained the dominant view of organized Christendom until the 17th century. During that century a major change in western thought took place. This change developed into an intellectual revolution. It caused many to reject Augustine's amillennial interpretation of the universe and history.[47]

Two aspects of the intellectual revolution prompted this rejection. First, a new interest in science focused man's attention upon the material universe and his ability to control nature. This clashed with Augustine's view that interest in the material universe was carnal. For example, Francis Bacon attacked the Augustinian conviction that any attempt to control or understand nature was the work of Satan.[48]

Second, European intellectuals became intensely interested in a *literal* understanding of the universe. They focused attention upon literal measurements, literal quantities, and literal calculations. This conflicted with the allegorical interpretation of the universe which characterized the Augustinian approach. The allegorical approach was seriously discredited when its interpretation of the nature of the heavens was proved to be mistaken by discoveries made through the use of the telescope.[49]

Through time this new concern with literalism as opposed to allegory spread to biblical scholars. Joseph Mede (1586-1638), a prominent Anglican Church Bible scholar, pioneered the return to the literal interpretation of the "Kingdom of God" passages in the Bible. As a result, he "concluded that the Scriptures held the promise of a literal Kingdom of God,"[50] and that this Kingdom would come in the future. This conclusion prompted him to adopt the premillennial view of the early Church.[51] Other scholars began to follow his example.[52]

The Development Of Postmillennialism

Some 17th-century Bible scholars who became convinced that the Bible promises a literal, future Kingdom of God did not adopt the premillennial view of the early Church. Instead, they developed the third major view concerning the Kingdom of God which has been held during the history of the Church.[53] That view has been called Postmillennialism (also called progressive Millennialism by some).[54]

The person credited with pioneering the development of the postmillennial view is Daniel Whitby (1638-1726) of England.[55] In spite of the fact that as a liberal Unitarian he was condemned for heresy, his view concerning the Kingdom of God became popular. Walvoord explains the reason:

> His views on the millennium would probably have never been perpetuated if they had not been so well keyed to the thinking of the times. The rising tide of intellectual freedom, science, and philosophy, coupled with humanism, had enlarged the concept of human progress and painted a bright picture of the future. Whitby's view of a coming golden age for the church was just what people wanted to hear."[56]

Postmillennialists were optimistic concerning the course of history. They believed that in spite of periodic conflicts and struggles, the ultimate progress of history is upward, eventually all problems will be solved, and time will be climaxed with a golden, utopian age.[57] This future time of blessing will not occur, through the supernatural intervention of Christ into world history at His Second Coming. Instead, it will come by a gradual process through human effort.[58]

Two Kinds Of Postmillennialism

Through time two major types of Postmillennialism developed. The first could be called conservative Postmillennialism. It was advocated by people who believed the Scriptures to be the inspired Word of God. They were convinced that the Old Testament prophecies concerning a future age of peace and righteousness must be fulfilled literally during the course of this earth's history. As God's people spread the gospel, eventually the whole world will be Christianized and brought into subjection to that message.

Thus, society will be transformed primarily through the efforts of the Church's ministering in the power of the Holy Spirit; however, civilization, science, and political agencies will play a role in this transformation as well. This means that the Church will play the key role in bringing in the future Kingdom of God foretold in the Bible. Christ will not be physically present on earth to rule from a literal, earthly throne. Instead, He will rule from Heaven while seated at the right hand of God. Thus, the throne promised to Him in the Scriptures is the Father's throne in Heaven. Christ's Second Coming will occur at the close of the Millennium as the crowning event of that golden age. In conjunction with the Second Coming there will be a general resurrection of all the dead, a general judgment of all human beings, and the end of the world, and then the future eternal state will begin.[59]

Jonathan Edwards (1703-58), a major leader of the *Great Awakening* in America during the 18th century, and Charles Hodge (1797-1878), the great Princeton theologian during the 19th century, were advocates of conservative Postmillennialism.[60],[61]

Edwards was convinced that the discovery and settlement of the New World was significant with regard to the establishment of the Millennium. During the 19th century many Protestant pastors expressed the belief that America would play the key role in leading the rest of the world in ushering in the Kingdom of God on earth.[62]

> In a typical utterance, a leading Presbyterian minister of the 1840s, Samuel H. Cox, told an English audience that, "in America, the state of society is without parallel in universal history...I really believe that God has got America within anchorage, and that upon that arena, He intends to display his prodigies for the millennium."[63]

This kind of postmillennial thinking aided the spread of America's 19th-century doctrine of *Manifest Destiny*.[64] Preachers declared that America obviously had been given a divine mandate to bring the whole continent from shore to shore under its jurisdiction so that from that base it could lead the world into the Millennium.

Postmillennialism also gave great impetus to the 19th-century American movement to abolish slavery. Many Christians regarded the Civil War as a battle of righteousness against this evil of slavery in society and, therefore, as an instrument to bring the world one step closer to the establishment of the Kingdom of God on earth. This was evidenced by the fact that the postmillennial hymn written by the Christian abolitionist, Julia Ward Howe, was called "The Battle Hymn of the Republic" (the Republic of America) and declared that God, His day, and His truth were marching on while men died to make men free.[65]

The second kind of Postmillennialism which developed could be called liberal Postmillennialism. It was very prevalent during the late 19th and early 20th centuries. In common with conservative Postmillennialism, it shared great optimism concerning the upward progress of history. It too was convinced that a future golden age (the Kingdom of God) would be established on earth.[66]

In spite of this common bond, liberal Postmillennialism differed radically from conservative Postmillennialism in several areas. It rejected the idea of the sinfulness of man and asserted that man is inherently good (not perfect, but good). It was convinced that man is perfectible and that human perfection will be attained through proper education, the improvement of man's environment, and the natural process of evolution. Liberal Postmillennialism had total confidence in the ability of man and science to correct all problems through the course of time.

This form of Postmillennialism rejected the deity of Christ. It declared that He was the greatest human being who ever lived, perhaps even the first perfect man, but certainly not God incarnated in human flesh. According to liberalism, Jesus was the example which all humans should follow in their move toward perfection.

Liberal Postmillennialism rejected the substitutionary atonement of Jesus Christ. Since man is not sinful by nature, he does not need a substitute to pay his penalty for sin. According to this view, instead of Jesus being a Savior from sin, He was the greatest teacher of ethics who ever lived.

Because liberalism rejected the substitutionary atonement of Christ, it also rejected the gospel of personal redemption from sin. In place of this gospel, which is revealed in the Bible, it substituted another message which it called the *social gospel*.[67] According to this message, personal redemption from sin has nothing to do with the establishing of the Millennium. The social gospel declared that the total mission of the Church is the redemption of society from all of its social evils (such as war, poverty, racism, injustice, disease, inequality, etc.). The Church is to accomplish this by bringing society into conformity with the ethical teachings of Christ by teaching the universal Fatherhood of God and universal brotherhood of man and by cooperating with science and the governmental, educational, charitable, labor, and other institutions of man.

Contrary to conservative Postmillennialism, which taught that society will be transformed primarily through the efforts of the Church's spreading the gospel of personal redemption from sin in the power of the Holy Spirit, liberal Postmillennialism asserted that the Kingdom of God will be established on earth through the Church and other human institutions using totally natural, humanly devised means.[68]

Prominent advocates of the liberal postmillennial view in America were Walter Rauschenbusch (1861-1918), a German

Baptist minister who served as Professor of New Testament and Professor of Church History at Rochester Theological Seminary and wrote such books as *Christianizing the Social Order* and *The Theology for the Social Gospel*, and Shirley Jackson Case (1872-1947), an American Baptist theologian who held the positions of Professor of New Testament Interpretation, Professor of History of Early Christianity, and Dean of the Divinity School at the University of Chicago and authored such books as *The Millennial Hope* and *The Christian Philosophy of History*.[69],[70],[71]

The gift of the Statue of Liberty to the United States in 1886 was, in essence, an expression of liberal Postmillennialism. The men of the Third Republic of France who conceived, designed, built, and presented the statue were liberal in their political outlook. They were convinced of several things: that the monarchies of Europe had oppressed their peoples for many centuries, that the American and French Revolutions were indicators that this oppressive yoke was about to be thrown off by the peoples of many nations, that personal liberty through governments of democracy was the wave of the future, and that America in particular was leading the rest of the world toward the future golden age of liberty through democracy. The fact that they were convinced that personal liberty was the wave of the future is indicated by the full title which they assigned to the statue: Liberty Enlightening The World. The fact that they determined to give the statue to the United States is evidence that they considered America to be the leader of the rest of the world toward the age of liberty through democracy.[72]

The Popularity And Decline Of Postmillennialism

From the time of its early development in the 17th century until the 20th century, Postmillennialism increased in popularity until it became "one of the most important and influential millennial theories. It was probably the dominant Protestant eschatology of the nineteenth century and was embraced by Unitarian, Arminian, and Calvinist alike."[73] It seemed to fit the optimistic spirit of the times. The rise of new democracies, the greater abundance of material goods and rising standard of living made possible by the industrial revolution in the west, the major discoveries in the fields of medicine, transportation, and communication, the rise of many new colleges and universities, and the relative peace maintained by Great Britain around the world for almost 100 years during the 19th century all made it appear that man was, indeed, on the verge of entering an unprecedented golden age of history. On the surface it appeared that Postmillennialism was the correct view of eschatology.

The optimism of Postmillennialism was dealt a severe blow, however, with the outbreak of World War I in 1914. Never before had the world seen a war of such magnitude involving so many nations. Science, which was supposed to help man usher in the age of peace and righteousness, now provided him with new tools with which to destroy great masses of humanity and thereby demonstrate his depraved nature more vividly than in the past. As a result, some theologians, such as Karl Barth, began to reject the concept of the inherent goodness of man which they had been taught by liberal theologians. Barth began to declare that man is sinful by nature and that the liberal view does not fit reality.

Postmillennialism recovered somewhat from the blow of World War I by asserting that this conflict would teach man an unforgettable lesson concerning the futility of war. Many pastors urged the men of their congregations to fight in this war that would end all wars and thereby play a role in permanently saving Christian civilization from destruction.

In line with this thinking, President Woodrow Wilson crusaded to enter the United States into this conflict in order "to make the world 'safe for democracy.' "[74]

After World War I ended, President Wilson tried to make the postmillennial dream of permanent peace a reality by laboring hard to establish the League of Nations. The purpose of the League was to provide the nations of the world with the means of settling differences peaceably without going to war with each other. This was to be accomplished by the representatives of the nations discussing and settling differences in the League meetings.

In spite of what appeared to be a decent recovery by Postmillennialism from the blow of World War I, further events of the 20th century proved to be very unkind to that optimistic millennial view. The League of Nations failed to accomplish its purpose and collapsed after a few years. Much of the world suffered a difficult economic depression during the 1930s. Nazi power tried to annihilate an entire nation of people through the practice of genocide. World War II, which proved to be even more horrible and of greater magnitude than World War I, began in the late 1930s. Man was catapulted into the atomic age with the development of weapons which gave him the potential of blowing himself and all of civilization into oblivion. The outlook on life expressed through western music, art, literature, philosophy, and some theology became increasingly pessimistic in the years after World War I.

For many people the optimistic view of the future, which characterized much of the western world through World War I, did not fit the harsh realities of the world. As a result, they rejected Postmillennialism, and it almost died. In the years immediately following World War II, almost no people, including students of the Bible, advocated that view of the

Millennium. During that time one of the few proponents of the conservative postmillennial view was Loraine Boettner (his book, *The Millennium*, was published in 1958).[75]

The next chapter will examine further historical developments affecting all three major views of the Millennium.

THIRTEEN

THE REVIVAL OF MILLENNIAL VIEWS

Four Stages of Development

D uring the history of the Church, views concerning the Millennium (the Kingdom of God foretold in such passages as Daniel 2 and 7) have gone through four stages of development. The first three stages were early Premillennialism and its rejection, the development of Amillennialism and its rejection, and the development of Postmillennialism and its rejection. These three stages were examined in the previous chapter.

In spite of the fact that all three millennial views have suffered a rejection, each also has experienced a revival. This revival constitutes the fourth stage of the history of millennial views, which will be examined in this chapter.

The Revival Of Premillennialism

Although early Premillennialism was rejected by the major part of organized Christendom by the fifth century, it continued to be advocated periodically throughout the centuries by certain individuals and groups. These advocates usually constituted a small minority, and some of them became quite radical and hyperemotional in their practice. As a result, the majority of professing Christians continued to regard Premillennialism as insignificant and fanatical.

Despite these negative associations, Premillennialism began to experience a significant revival during the 19th century. This revived form differed considerably from the radical expressions of earlier centuries. Ernest R. Sandeen, a 20th-century historian, stated that "Unlike many of the earlier reawakenings of Millenarianism, however, these modern American apocalyptic groups possessed no revolutionary potential."[1]

Adolph Harnack, a leading Church historian of the 19th century, declared, "in recent times an exceedingly mild type of 'academic' chiliasm has been developed from a belief in the verbal inspiration of the Bible."[2] Harnack's comment emphasized two traits of the revived Premillennialism of his century. First, it was characterized by an organized, systematic study of the biblical data concerning the Kingdom of God, instead of by fanatical emotionalism. Second, it was based upon a strong belief in the divine inspiration and authority of the Scriptures (even including their words).

Concerning this second characteristic of premillennial belief, Sandeen commented, "Without the influence of the Bible, no connected millennial tradition would exist....As long as Christians accept the texts of the Bible as the Word of God, the tradition will endure."[3]

The 19th-century revival of Premillennialism began in Great Britain primarily through the influence of the Plymouth Brethren (who were founded around 1830) and one of their key leaders, John Nelson Darby (1800-1882).[4]

To the surprise of many, this revival of Premillennialism rose suddenly and prospered considerably in America in the latter third of the 19th century. This was especially true of dispensational Premillennialism.[5] Weber wrote,

> After the Civil War the last thing most American evangelicals expected was a resurgence of Premillennialism. Belief in Christ's personal return to set

up his earthly kingdom had always had its faithful witnesses in the churches, but few people imagined that it would ever again be able to attract a significant number of adherents scattered throughout the evangelical denominations or isolated in premillennial denominations.[6]

A significant number of influential Christian leaders were advocates of the premillennial view. For example, D. L. Moody (1837-1899), the greatest evangelist during the latter third of the 19th century, was convinced of the truthfulness of Premillennialism. The same was true of almost every major evangelist who succeeded him, such as J. Wilbur Chapman (1859-1918), Reuben A. Torrey (1856-1928), and Billy Sunday (1862-1935).[7]

Several key missions leaders were premillennial by conviction. Among them were Robert Speer (1867-1947), who served as secretary of the Presbyterian Board of Foreign Missions for 46 years; A. T. Pierson (1837-1911), editor of the *Missionary Review of the World* for 23 years; and A. B. Simpson (1843-1919), the Presbyterian minister who founded the Christian and Missionary Alliance.[8]

Premillennialism was taught from the pulpit by prominent pastors, such as James H. Brookes (1830-1897), pastor of Walnut Street Presbyterian Church in St. Louis; A. J. Gordon (1836-1895), pastor of the Clarendon Street Baptist Church in Boston; and C. I. Scofield (1843-1921), pastor of the First Congregational Church of Dallas and the Trinitarian Congregational Church of Northfield, Massachusetts.[9]

The Bible school movement, which began in the late 1800s, significantly aided the revival and spread of Premillennialism. The earliest Bible school in America was founded by T. DeWitt Talmage in Brooklyn, New York, in 1870. A. B. Simpson started the Missionary Training College in New

York City in 1883. Moody Bible Institute began in Chicago in 1886. By 1940, 78 such schools had been founded in key cities all across America. Almost all of these schools were premillennial in their teaching.

The late 19th century witnessed the rise of the Bible and prophecy conference movements, both of which emphasized the premillennial faith. The best known of the early Bible conferences was the Niagara Bible Conference which began in 1875.[10] The first official prophecy conference was conducted by premillennialists at Holy Trinity Episcopal Church in New York City in October 1878.[11] Other Bible and prophecy conferences began to be held at many locations.

The faith missions movement (independent or nondenominational missions) also began in the late 1800s. A number of these new missions propagated premillennial teaching. One such mission was the Central American Mission (now CAM International) which was founded under the leadership of C. I. Scofield in Dallas, Texas, in 1890.[12] Those missions which were founded primarily to minister to Jews (such as The American Board of Missions to the Jews and The Friends of Israel Gospel Ministry, Inc.) have been consistently premillennial.

Various kinds of literature have provided widespread exposure for the revived Premillennialism. Magazines, such as *Truth or Testimony for Christ* (published by James H. Brookes for 23 years in the late 1800s),[13] *Our Hope* (edited by Arno C. Gaebelein from 1894 to 1945),[14] *Israel My Glory* (produced by The Friends of Israel Gospel Ministry, Inc.), and *Moody Monthly*, have played a key role. Study Bibles, such as the Scofield Reference Bible (first published in 1909) and the Ryrie Study Bible (1978), have made a major impact. Theological journals, such as *Bibliotheca Sacra* (published by Dallas Theological Seminary), and books such as the monumental three-volume *The Theocratic Kingdom* (by George

N. H. Peters, a Lutheran scholar who lived from 1825 to 1909),[15] *The Basis of the Premillennial Faith* (Charles C. Ryrie), *The Millennial Kingdom* (John F. Walvoord), and *Things to Come* (J. Dwight Pentecost), have given scholarly presentations of the premillennial view.

Premillennialists of the 20th century founded several theological seminaries to train pastors, missionaries, Bible teachers, and other Christian workers in the premillennial faith. Among these were Dallas Theological Seminary (founded in 1924), Grace Theological Seminary (founded in 1937), Talbot Theological Seminary, and Western Conservative Baptist Seminary.

A number of denominations or church fellowships which were predominantly premillennial were formed. Examples of these were the General Association of Regular Baptists, the Conservative Baptist Association, the Independent Fundamental Churches of America, the Plymouth Brethren, and the Grace Brethren.

The revived Premillennialism played a key role in the Fundamentalist movement of the late 19th and 20th centuries. Sandeen stated that premillennialists "contributed directly to the rise of the biblically oriented and conservative movement known as Fundamentalism."[16]

The Revival Of Amillennialism

The postmillennialists of the 17th to early 20th centuries interpreted the Kingdom of God passages in the Bible literally. As a result, they were convinced that the Bible promises a literal, future Kingdom of God on earth. They believed, however, that that kingdom would be established through human effort, not through divine intervention into history.

As noted earlier, the tragedies of the 20th century demonstrated that the optimistic postmillennial view did not fit the harsh realities of the world. As a result, most postmillennialists became so disillusioned with their view that they abandoned it. Now they had two major alternatives open to them. They could turn to the premillennial view. Such a turn would have permitted them to hold onto the literal interpretation of the Kingdom of God passages in the Bible and their conviction that the Bible promised a literal, future Kingdom of God on earth, but it would have required them to reject their belief concerning how that kingdom would be established. They would have had to believe that it would be established through divine intervention into history, not through human effort.

The other alternative open to the disenchanted postmillennialists was a turn to the amillennial view. This turn would have required them to reject the literal interpretation of the Kingdom of God passages in the Bible and their conviction that the Bible promised a literal, future Kingdom of God on earth. The rejection of both these things was characteristic of Amillennialism.

Most postmillennialists (conservative and liberal alike) took the alternative of turning to the amillennial view. Since the majority of Protestants in the early 20th century had been postmillennial by conviction, this turn constituted a major revival for the amillennial view. During the late 1950s Walvoord wrote the following concerning this revival:

> In the last two decades there has been an evident resurgence in Amillennialism. The converts have come from many sources. Those who had become skeptical about a millennium on earth to be achieved through Christian influence and the church found it a natural conclusion that their error lay in taking too seriously the glowing prophecies of the Old Testament of a kingdom of righteousness and peace on earth. There were no signs of such

an era on the horizon, and both Christians and non-Christians were talking darkly of the end of civilization and a third and final world war in which man would destroy himself. It seemed in the spirit of the times to conclude that there would be no millennium on earth and that freedom from sin and war was to be found only in heaven. While the downward course of the modern world was no embarrassment to premillenarians who had been preaching about such a trend for years, the church as a whole was unwilling to admit any accuracy in the premillennial view.[17]

Thus, the majority of Protestants converted to the amillennial view. When this circumstance is combined with the fact that the Roman Catholic and Eastern Orthodox Churches were consistently amillennial, it can be seen that Amillennialism had become the majority view of organized Christendom by the middle of the 20th century.

The Revival Of Postmillennialism

During the years immediately following World War II, it appeared that the postmillennial view would be dead forever. Almost none advocated it. For all practical purposes, the struggle over which millennial view was correct was waged entirely between Premillennialism and Amillennialism. However, contrary to what was expected, the times since the late 1960s have witnessed a revival of the postmillennial view in different forms.

One form of the new Postmillennialism has been radically secular and anti-Christian in nature. Advocates of this form are convinced that it is possible for man to usher in a utopian golden age upon this earth. Some believe that this can be accomplished by science through such means as genetic engineering. Others are convinced that proper social planning, together with conditioning of the youth to conform to that planning, will bring it about. Some "claim that a *reversal* of all Christian values is necessary for the breaking-in of the" golden age.[18] For example, Professor Charles A. Reich of Yale, in his best-selling book *The Greening of America* (published in 1970), indicated that "such things as drug use, contempt for productive work, sexual licentiousness, and pornography" may be the tools which will usher in utopia.[19] Thomas J. J. Altizer, one of the God-is-dead theologians, asserted that the golden age of history will not come until human beings admit that the God of Scripture is dead, reverse all biblical morality, and acclaim themselves divine.[20]

Another form of the new Postmillennialism differs drastically from the radical secular one. It is conservative in nature and is advocated by spokesmen within the Reformed-Covenant Theology tradition. This new form has been called *theonomy*. The term *theonomy* comes from two Greek words which mean *God* and *law*. This term is an accurate designation for this new form of Postmillennialism, for theonomists claim "that the Mosaic law, more or less in its entirety, constitutes a continuing norm for mankind and that it is the duty of the civil magistrate to enforce it, precepts and penalties alike."[21] Thus, according to this view, capital punishment should be administered today to homosexuals, drunkards, and rebellious teen-aged children.[22]

The key passage of theonomy is Matthew 5:17-19. On the basis of this passage, theonomists assert that the Mosaic Law is binding upon all human beings forever and that there is a "public obligation to promote and enforce obedience to God's law in society."[23]

Theonomists believe that Matthew 5:13-16 presents the Church with "a mandate for the complete social transformation of the entire world."[24] The Church is to play the key role in this transformation by spreading the gospel throughout the world, taking over the function of government, and enforcing the Mosaic Law. Thus, Chilton stated, "Our goal is world dominion under Christ's Lordship, a 'world takeover' if you will; but our strategy begins with reformation, reconstruction of the church. From that will flow social and political reconstruction, indeed a flowering of Christian civilization."[25] Again he said, "The Christian goal for the world is the universal development of biblical theocratic republics, in which every area of life is redeemed and placed under the Lordship of Jesus Christ and the rule of God's law."[26]

Another theonomist declared that "the saints must prepare to take over the world's governments and its courts."[27]

Theonomists optimistically believe that "As the gospel progresses throughout the world it will win, and win, and win, until all kingdoms become the kingdoms of our Lord and of His Christ."[28]

Bahnsen stated that "The gospel...shall convert the vast majority of the world to Christ and bring widespread obedience to His kingdom rule," and that "the church will grow to fill the earth, and that Christianity will become the dominant principle."[29]

This optimistic belief makes theonomy a genuine form of Postmillennialism. Theonomists openly identify their movement with that millennial view. Bahnsen asserted that "The thing that distinguishes the biblical postmillennialist then from amillennialism and premillennialism is his belief that Scripture teaches the success of the great commission in this age of the church."[30]

Rushdoony wrote,

Postmillennialism thus believes that man must be saved, and that his regeneration is the starting point for a mandate to exercise dominion in Christ's name over every area of life and thought. Postmillennialism in its classic form does not neglect the church and it does not neglect also to work for a Christian state and school, for the sovereignty and crown rights of the King over individuals, families, institutions, arts, scientists, and all things else. More, it holds that God has provided the way for this conquest: His Law.[31]

The major publication advocating theonomy is the *Journal of Christian Reconstruction.* Organizations which propagate this view are the Chalcedon Ministries, Christianity and Civilization, and the Geneva Divinity School Press of Tyler, Texas. Major spokesmen for the movement are Greg L. Bahnsen, James B. Jordan, Gary North, Rousas John Rushdoony, and Norman Shepherd.[32]

Another voice for a conservative form of Postmillennialism is John Jefferson Davis, Associate Professor of Systematic Theology and Christian Ethics at Gordon-Conwell Theological Seminary. In his book, *Christ's Victorious Kingdom, Postmillennialism Reconsidered* (1987), Davis presents a fresh examination of this millennial view and deals with its implications for missionary activity and social reform.[33]

FOURTEEN

THE KINGDOM OF GOD CONCEPT IN THE SCRIPTURES

Preliminary Considerations

T he last few chapters have surveyed the history of millennial views within organized Christendom. They demonstrated the fact that Premillennialism was the original view of the Church.

The fact that Premillennialism was the initial view of the Church is quite significant because it favors the conclusion that Premillennialism is the correct millennial view. It should be noted, however, that correctness of a view is not proven conclusively by the fact that it was the original view. Initial impressions and conclusions of human beings in any realm of knowledge can be incorrect. Because this is true, the ultimate test of correctness for any view in the realm of theology is not the question of it being the original view, but the question of its agreement with the Scriptures. In order for a view concerning the Millennium to be correct, it must agree with the teaching of the Bible.

The previous chapter which dealt with the Davidic Covenant and its fulfillment presented evidence that the premillennial view of the Millennium agrees with the teaching of the Bible. Further evidence to the same effect is found in an examination of the Kingdom of God concept in the Scriptures. The purpose of the present chapter is to examine that concept.

The Basis Of The Kingdom Of God Concept In The Scriptures

The Kingdom of God concept in the Bible is derived from the fact that God is sovereign. This is indicated by David's great expression recorded in 1 Chronicles 29:11-12:

> Thine, O LORD, is the greatness, and the power, and the glory, and the victory, and the majesty; for all that is in the heaven and in the earth is thine. Thine is the kingdom, O LORD, and thou art exalted as head above all. Both riches and honor come of thee, and thou reignest over all; and in thine hand is power and might; and in thine hand it is to make great, and to give strength unto all.

In this expression David declared at least three significant things concerning God. First, God has sovereign power or authority to rule. Second, He has a realm of subjects (all that is in the heavenly and earthly realms) over which to exercise His sovereign rule. Third, He actually exercises His sovereign rule over that realm. All three of these things are essential in order to have a kingdom. Since God in His sovereignty possesses or does all these things, David declared that God has a Kingdom. The sovereignty of God, then, is the basis of the Kingdom of God concept in the Bible.

The sovereignty of God is also the basis of the biblical philosophy of history. This was noted in an earlier chapter. Since both the Kingdom of God concept in the Bible and the biblical philosophy of history are based upon the sovereignty of God, it would appear that both are related significantly to each other. Indeed, the Kingdom of God concept is the heart of the biblical philosophy of history and, therefore, is the central theme of the Bible.

Distinctions In The Kingdom Of God Concept In The Scriptures

As the Bible deals with the Kingdom of God concept, it presents distinctions in that concept which at first appear to be contradictions. There are at least three such distinctions.

First, there is a distinction of *time*. Some Scriptures present the Kingdom of God as an entity *already in existence* from long ago: "The LORD hath prepared his throne in the heavens, and his kingdom ruleth over all" (Ps. 103:19; cf. Lam. 5:19).

By contrast, other Scriptures indicate that the Kingdom of God is to *come in the future*; it is not here yet: "And in the days of these kings shall the God of heaven set up a kingdom, which shall never be destroyed" (Dan. 2:44; cf. 7:13-14, 27). When Jesus was present in the world during His first coming, He taught His disciples to pray that the Kingdom of God would come (Mt. 6:10).

Second, there is a distinction of *scope*. Some Scriptures present the Kingdom of God as being *universal in scope*. It has the entire universe as its realm. As noted earlier, David said to God, "all that is in the heaven and in the earth is thine. Thine is the kingdom, O LORD, and thou art exalted as head above all...and thou reignest over all" (1 Chr. 29:11-12). In Psalm 103:19 David declared that God's "kingdom ruleth over all" (cf. Ps. 135:6).

Paul stated that God is "Lord of heaven and earth" (Acts 17:24).

By contrast, other Scriptures present the Kingdom of God as being *earthly in scope*. It has just the earth as its realm. In Daniel 2:35, 44-45, the stone, which represented the future Kingdom which God will establish, filled the whole earth. According to Zechariah 14:4, 9, when Messiah stands on the Mount of Olives at His Second Coming, "the LORD shall be king over all the earth." John foresaw creatures of God in the future Tribulation period talking about the kingdom (singular in the Greek text) of the world becoming the Kingdom of God and His Christ (Rev. 11:15).

In Daniel 7:13-14, 27, the future Kingdom, which God will give to the Son of Man who comes with the clouds of Heaven and to the saints, is described as being "under the whole heaven."

The third distinction in the Kingdom of God concept is *administration*. Some Scriptures present the Kingdom of God as being God's rule administered *directly* by Him *over any or all parts of the universe*. No human mediator administers the divine rule on behalf of God. God gave a classic example of this direct administration of His Kingdom rule when He bound powerful King Nebuchadnezzar with a humiliating form of mental illness and thereby removed him from his throne (Dan. 4). No human agent caused Nebuchadnezzar's insanity on behalf of God. God did it directly. The purpose of this sovereign act was to demonstrate the fact "that the Most High ruleth in the kingdom of men" (v. 17).

At the end of his negative experience, Nebuchadnezzar acknowledged the fact that his mental illness was an expression of the sovereign rule of God's Kingdom (v. 34). He described the directness of God's Kingdom rule as follows: "he doeth according to his will in the army of heaven, and among the inhabitants of the earth, and none can stay his hand, or say unto him, What doest thou?" (v. 35). Nebuchadnezzar called God "the King of heaven" (v. 37).

God gave another demonstration of the direct administration of His Kingdom rule when He killed 185,000 Assyrian soldiers who were threatening Jerusalem (2 Ki. 19). He did this in one night and without the aid of any human agents. Concerning this sovereign administration of His Kingdom rule He declared,

Surely as I have thought, so shall it come to pass; and as I have purposed, so shall it stand: That I will break the Assyrian in my land...This is the purpose that is purposed upon the whole earth, and this is the hand that is stretched out upon all the nations. For the LORD of hosts hath purposed, and who shall annul it? And his hand is stretched out, and who shall turn it back? (Isa. 14:24-27).

By contrast, other Scriptures present the Kingdom of God as being God's rule administered *indirectly* through a human mediator *just over the earth.* Psalm 2:6-9 portrays God's establishing Messiah as King to rule over the nations and all parts of the earth. The fact that Messiah will administer God's rule on His behalf is indicated by two things. First, God calls Messiah "my king" (v. 6). Second, any rebellion against Messiah will also be rebellion against God (vv. 2-3) and will bring God's wrath (vv. 4-5).

Daniel 7:13-14 depicts God's giving the Son of Man a Kingdom over which to rule. This Kingdom will consist of all people, nations, and languages (v. 14) and will be "under the whole heaven" (limited to this earth) [v.27]. A parallel passage (Dan. 2:44) indicates that this Kingdom which is given by God to the Son of Man is God's Kingdom, for it declares that this Kingdom is set up by the God of Heaven. A comparison of Daniel 2:35 with verses 44 and 45 shows that this Kingdom of God will fill the whole earth. Thus, Daniel 2 and 7 are describing an earthly Kingdom of God in which God's rule is administered indirectly through a human mediator, the Son of Man who comes with the clouds of Heaven.

Similar concepts are presented in Revelation 11:15, which talks about the kingdom of the world becoming the Kingdom of God and of His Christ and then declares that *one* of these Persons ("he" — singular) will reign. Revelation 19 and 20 clearly indicate that Christ is that one person who will come to earth to reign over this Kingdom of God. Here again is the picture of an earthly Kingdom of God in which the rule of God is administered indirectly through a human representative, Christ.

There are, then, three significant distinctions in the biblical Kingdom of God concept: the distinction of *time* (the Kingdom of God has been in existence for a long time, but it also has not yet started); the distinction of *scope* (the Kingdom of God is universal in scope, and yet it is just earthly in scope); and the distinction of *administration* (the Kingdom of God is the rule of God administered directly by Him over any or all parts of the universe, but it also is the rule of God administered indirectly through a human mediator just over the earth).

The Explanation Of These Distinctions In The Kingdom Of God Concept

In spite of how it may appear, these distinctions are not contradictions. Instead, they are indicators of the fact that the Kingdom of God has at least two aspects or expressions.

The Universal Kingdom of God is the first aspect or expression of the Kingdom of God. The Universal Kingdom of God is the rule of God over the entire universe (including the earth) and everything in the universe.

Ever since God created the universe, He has reigned as sovereign Lord over it. Thus, Paul declared that the God who created things "is Lord of heaven and earth" (Acts 17:24). This Universal Kingdom rule of God, then, has been in existence since long ago, and it will always be in existence.

The dispensations are the different ways in which God administers His Universal Kingdom rule over the earth during earth's history. In an earlier chapter, it was noted that a dispensation is a particular way of God's administering His rule over the world as He progressively works out His purpose for world history. It could be said that each dispensation is a particular expression or phase of the Universal Kingdom rule of God over the earthly province of His Universal Kingdom. For example, the dispensation of grace is the present expression or phase of the Universal Kingdom rule of God over the earth.

Sometimes God administers His Universal Kingdom rule directly (not through a mediator), and sometimes He administers it indirectly through a mediator or representative.

Because the Universal Kingdom of God is His rule over the entire universe, it is the broad aspect or expression of the Kingdom of God.

The Theocratic Kingdom of God is the second aspect or expression of the Kingdom of God. A theocracy is the form of government in which the rule of God is administered through a mediator or representative. In light of the nature of a theocracy, and in light of the biblical teaching concerning this aspect of the Kingdom of God, several conclusions can be drawn concerning the Theocratic Kingdom of God.

First, the Theocratic Kingdom of God is a more narrow or limited aspect of the Kingdom of God than is the Universal Kingdom of God. This is so because the Theocratic Kingdom of God is only one expression or phase of the Univeral Kingdom.

Second, the Theocratic Kingdom of God is restricted to God's rule over the earth; it does not involve His rule over the entire universe. By contrast, the Universal Kingdom of God is the rule of God over the entire universe (including the earth).

Third, the Theocratic Kingdom of God is restricted to the indirect administration of God's rule through a human mediator or representative (through an Adam); it does not involve God's direct administration of His rule. By contrast, the Universal Kingdom of God involves both the indirect and direct administration of God's rule.

Fourth, the Theocratic Kingdom of God is restricted just to those times when God has an Adam administering His rule over the entire earth. There are only two such time periods for this present earth: the time between man's creation and fall and the time of the future Millennium.

Prior to the fall of man, the Theocratic Kingdom of God existed on planet Earth. God made Adam the human administrator of His rule over the earthly province of His Universal Kingdom. Adam did not obtain his position or authority on his own; it was given to him by God (Gen. 1:26, 28; Ps. 8:3-9). Thus, it was God's rule that was administered over the world system by Adam from the time of his creation to the time of his fall. Therefore, during the first dispensation of the Universal Kingdom rule of God over the earth, that rule was in the form of a theocracy.

Tragically, things did not continue that way. Satan persuaded Adam to defect from God (Gen. 3). Through this fall of man away from God, God lost His representative who was to administer His rule over the world system. As a result, the Theocratic Kingdom phase of His Universal Kingdom rule of the earth was also lost.

When Adam defected from God, he handed over to Satan the authority to rule the world system which God had entrusted to him. Satan specifically declared that this was so in Luke 4:6. As a result of his getting Adam to defect from God, Satan usurped the rule of the world system away from God. Thus, the lost theocracy was replaced by a satanocracy.

Satan's rule has continued to dominate the world system since the fall of man. Several things indicate that this is so. During His first coming, Jesus called Satan "the prince of this world" more than once (Jn. 12:31; 14:30; 16:11). The word translated *prince* means *ruler*.[1] Satan had authority to offer the rule of the world system to Jesus (Lk. 4:5-6). Paul called Satan "the god of this age" (2 Cor. 4:4, literal translation), and John declared that "the whole world lies in the evil one" (1 Jn. 5:19, literal translation). James warned that whoever is a friend of the present world system is the enemy of God (Jas. 4:4). The Scriptures assert that believers are strangers and pilgrims on the earth (Heb. 11:13; 1 Pet. 2:11). Jesus indicated that His followers were not of the world system even though they were in it (Jn. 17:14-18). Peter warned believers in the world to be vigilant because their adversary, the devil, walks about like a roaring lion, seeking to devour them (1 Pet. 5:8-9). Thus, believers are in enemy territory while living in the present world system, for that system is ruled by God's great enemy.

It is important to note that even though Satan usurped the rule of the world system away from God when Adam fell, God's ownership of the earth and His Universal Kingdom rule over the earth did not end at that time. Only the Theocratic Kingdom phase of His Universal Kingdom rule of the earth ended at the fall of man. Other phases of His Universal Kingdom rule have been present on the earth since the fall. Thus, centuries after Adam's rebellion David could write, "The earth is the LORD's, and the fullness thereof" (Ps. 24:1), and God could declare, "the world is mine, and all the fullness thereof" (Ps. 50:12). In addition, as noted earlier, during the course of world history God has exhibited His continuing Universal Kingdom rule over the earth through such sovereign acts as His binding of King

Nebuchadnezzar with mental illness (Dan. 4). These sovereign acts have been for the purpose of demonstrating the fact "that the Most High ruleth in the kingdom of men" (Dan. 4:17).

Beginning immediately after the fall of Adam and continuing throughout Bible times, God promised that He would crush Satan and his rule of the world system, that He would cast Satan and his satanocracy out of the world, that He would accomplish this through a Redeemer-Messiah, Jesus Christ, and that He would restore His Theocratic Kingdom rule to the earth by turning over the rule of the whole world to Jesus who would function as the last Adam.

Following are examples of such prophetic promises. In Genesis 3:15 God indicated that a man-child, born of woman during world history, would crush Satan. In Psalm 2 God expressed His determination to establish His anointed One (His Messiah), His Son, as His King in Jerusalem and to turn over to Him the nations and the uttermost parts of the earth. He also declared that His King would crush the godless forces of the world. In Isaiah 9:6-7 God declared that a man-child, who would be born during history and who also would be called "The Mighty God," would rule a Kingdom government upon the throne of David. He clearly indicated that it would be the zeal of the Lord, not the zeal of man, which would bring this about. In Isaiah 11 God foretold that a descendant of Jesse would crush the wicked and rule righteously and faithfully in complete harmony with God, that animals would be completely tame and vegetarian in diet, and that the earth would be full of the knowledge of the Lord during that rule. In Daniel 7 God portrayed Himself giving the Son of Man a future Kingdom over which to rule in conjunction with the Son of Man's coming with the clouds of Heaven. God indicated that this Kingdom would consist of all the nations and peoples under the whole Heaven.

God sent the angel Gabriel to Mary to inform her that she would give birth to a man-child, who would be called Jesus and the Son of God and who would reign over a Kingdom upon the throne of David (Lk. 1). Jesus indicated that His death constituted a judgment of the godless world system and guaranteed the future casting out (the verb is future tense in the text) of Satan from the world (Jn. 12:31). Paul, writing several years after Jesus' death, declared that God would crush Satan in the future (the verb is future tense) [Rom. 16:20]. John declared that the Son of God came for the purpose of destroying the works of the devil (1 Jn. 3:8; cf. Heb. 2:14). Jesus declared that, as the Son of Man, He would come with the clouds of Heaven at His future Second Coming (Mt. 24:29-30), that He would then sit upon His throne (Mt. 25:31) and send the righteous into the Kingdom (Mt. 25:34), and that the earth would then experience its regeneration (Mt. 19:28). Peter asserted that the earth would experience the future times of refreshing and restitution of all things promised by God through the prophets when Jesus returns from Heaven at His Second Coming and is present on earth again (Acts 3:19-21). Paul called Jesus "the last Adam" (1 Cor. 15:45) and indicated that He would reign over a Kingdom (1 Cor. 15:24-25).

All of these promises indicate that God has a purpose for the history of this present earth. His purpose is to glorify Himself by demonstrating the fact that He alone is the sovereign God. Satan challenged the sovereign rule of God by usurping the rule of the world system away from Him through the defection of God's first Adam. God has determined to demonstrate His sovereignty by crushing Satan and his rule of the world system, casting Satan and his satanocracy out of the world, and by restoring His Theocratic Kingdom rule to the earth with Jesus administering that rule over the entire earth as the last Adam. Since the Theocratic Kingdom originally existed and was lost during this present earth's history, it is essential that God restore it during this same earth's history. If the history of this present earth ends without that restoration, God will be defeated by His great enemy during this course of history. Just as the Universal Kingdom rule of God over the earth during the first dispensation was in the form of a theocracy, so must the Universal Kingdom rule of God over the earth in the last dispensation be in the form of a theocracy if God is to accomplish His purpose for the history of this present earth.[2]

It is significant that the Book of The Revelation, which was the last book of the Bible written and, therefore, the capstone of all biblical revelation, portrays the following sequence of events: first, God's systematic attacks against the satanocracy through three series of judgments upon the earth during the Tribulation period (Rev. 6-18); second, the Second Coming of Jesus Christ to earth with the final crushing of Satan's forces (Rev. 19:11-21); third, the casting out of Satan from the earth and his imprisonment in the bottomless pit (Rev. 20:1-3); and, fourth, the Kingdom reign of Christ over this present earth for 1,000 years (the Millennium) [Rev. 20:4-6]. It is important to note that The Revelation portrays all these events taking place *before* the destruction of the present earth (Rev. 20:11). In other words, it portrays God's crushing Satan and his satanocracy, casting out Satan from the earth, and restoring His Theocratic Kingdom during this present earth's history. The fact that God would portray this sequence of events in the book which is the capstone of all biblical revelation would seem to indicate that He intends this sequence of events to play a key role in the great climax of the present earth's history and, therefore, in the fulfillment of His purpose for its history.

Conclusion

Only the premillennial view of the Millennium agrees with the Kingdom of God concept as it is presented in the Bible. The amillennial view does not agree with it, for Amillennialism rejects the concept of the restoration of the Theocratic Kingdom to this present earth during its history. The postmillennial view does not agree with it, for Postmillennialism rejects the concept that the Theocratic Kingdom will not be restored to this earth until Jesus Christ returns in His glorious Second Coming. According to Postmillennialism, Jesus will return in His glorious Second Coming at the very end of this present earth's history *after* the Theocratic Kingdom has been restored to earth through human effort.

FIFTEEN

THE BEGINNING AND NATURE OF THE CHURCH

The Problem Stated

Covenant Theology and Dispensational Theology disagree concerning two major matters related to the Church. Those two matters are the time the Church began and the nature of the Church. Both of these matters will be examined in this chapter.

The Time The Church Began

Covenant Theology declares that the Church began during Old Testament times. Some Covenant Theologians believe that it began during the days of Adam. For example, R. B. Kuiper wrote that it may be asserted that Adam and Eve "constituted the first Christian church."[1]

Other Covenant Theologians are convinced that the Church started when God established the Abrahamic Covenant with Abraham. One such theologian, Charles Hodge, stated, "The Church under the New Dispensation is identical with that under the Old. It is not a new Church but one and the same. It is the same olive tree (Rom. xi. 16-17). It is founded on the same covenant, the covenant made with Abraham."[2]

In contrast with the Covenant Theology view, Dispensational Theology declares that the Church did not begin until the Day of Pentecost of Acts 2. Thus, the Church did *not* exist in Old Testament times. Radmacher wrote that "the church did not come into functional existence until the day of Pentecost."[3] Although the Church was an essential part of God's plan for history which He determined in eternity past, God did not put that part of His plan into effect until ten days after His Son ascended from earth to Heaven.

The Nature Of The Church

Concerning the nature of the Church, Covenant Theology asserts that the Church is the continuing covenanted community of God's people throughout history. It consists of all people who have had the Covenant of Grace relationship with God regardless of the period of history in which they have lived. Thus, the Church is the same, in essence, throughout history. The earlier quotation of Charles Hodge clearly indicates that this was his understanding of the nature of the Church. Louis Berkhof, another prominent Covenant Theologian, wrote that "the Church existed in the old dispensation as well as in the new, and was essentially the same in both."[4]

It should be noted that the Covenant Theology view of the nature of the Church leads logically to several conclusions. Israel and the Church are the same; there are no distinctive groups of saints throughout history; all saints of all periods of history are members of the Church; since saints will be on earth during the Tribulation period, the Church will be on earth during the Tribulation, and there will be one general resurrection of dead saints at one time, not more than one resurrection of saints at different times.

In contrast with the Covenant Theology view of the nature of the Church, Dispensational Theology asserts that the Church consists only of those saved people who live between the Day of Pentecost of Acts 2 and the Rapture of the Church from the earth. Saints who died before the Day of Pentecost and people who become saved after the Rapture of the Church are never part of the Church. Thus, the Church consists of a distinctive group of saints who live during one particular period of history — namely, those saints who are baptized with the Spirit.

It is essential to note that the Dispensational Theology view of the nature of the Church also leads logically to several conclusions. Israel and the Church are not the same; there is something distinctive about the relationship of the Holy Spirit to saints between the Day of Pentecost and the Rapture of the Church; there are distinctions between groups of saints throughout history (Old Testament saints, Church saints, Tribulation saints, Millennial saints); the fact that saints will be on earth during the Tribulation period does not require the Church to be on earth during the Tribulation; and there will be more than one resurrection of dead saints at different times of history, not just one general resurrection of saints.

Evidence That The Church Did Not Exist In Old Testament Times But Began At Pentecost

The New Testament presents several lines of evidence to the effect that the Church did not begin until the Day of Pentecost. The first line of evidence is that the Church was not formed apart from the baptism with the Spirit, and Spirit baptism did not begin until the Day of Pentecost. In Colossians 1:18 and 24 Paul declared that the body of Christ is the Church. In 1 Corinthians 12:13 he indicated that all believers in Christ (Jew and Gentile alike) are placed into the body of Christ through Spirit baptism. Thus, Paul was teaching the necessity of Spirit baptism for the formation of the Church.

John the Baptist clearly indicated that he was not baptizing people with the Spirit in his time. Instead, he stated that Jesus would baptize with the Spirit in the future (Lk. 3:16). On the day of His ascension, Jesus declared that His believers should remain in Jerusalem for a few more days to receive the baptism with the Spirit to which John referred, which the Father had promised and about which Jesus had talked (Acts 1:4-5). The language of Jesus' statement implied that Spirit baptism had not yet begun historically and would not begin until a few days after His ascension. Acts 2 indicates that it began on the Day of Pentecost, ten days after Jesus' ascension.

On the basis of the statements by Paul, John the Baptist, and Jesus, two conclusions can be drawn. First, since Spirit baptism is necessary for the formation of the Church, and since Spirit baptism did not begin historically until the Day of Pentecost, the Church did not begin historically until the Day of Pentecost.

Second, on the Day of Pentecost the Holy Spirit began to be related to believers in Jesus Christ in ways in which He was not related to Old Testament believers. Certainly the Holy Spirit was at work in the world in some ways before the Day of Pentecost (cf. Gen. 6:3; Ex. 35:30-33; Num. 11:26-30; 24:2), but on Pentecost He came with some new ways of working which had not been present before. Thus, there is something distinctive about the relationship of the Holy Spirit to saints in the period of history since Pentecost. This is substantiated by other statements in the New Testament. On the last day of the Feast of Tabernacles, Jesus promised that the believer would have rivers of living water flowing out of his heart (Jn. 7:37-38). John explained Jesus' statement this way: "But this spoke he of the Spirit, whom they that believe on him should receive; for the Holy Spirit was not yet given, because Jesus was not yet glorified" (Jn. 7:39). John indicated that the Spirit would come in a new, distinctive sense after Jesus was glorified through His death, resurrection, and ascension (Jn. 12:16, 23-27; 17:1, 5; Phil. 2:8-9).

The night before Jesus was crucified He promised that after He returned to the Father in Heaven, the Father would send the Holy Spirit to His disciples (Jn. 14:2-4, 16-17, 26; 16:12-

16). He declared that the Spirit would not come while He was present on earth (Jn. 16:7). He also drew a clear distinction between the relationship of the Spirit with His disciples *before* His ascension and what it would be *after* His ascension: "for he dwelleth with you, and shall be in you" (Jn. 14:17).

The second line of evidence that the Church did not begin until Pentecost is Peter's assertion that something new began when the believers were baptized with the Spirit on Pentecost. Speaking of his experience at Cornelius' house (Acts 10), Peter said, "And as I began to speak, the Holy Spirit fell on them, as on us at the beginning. Then remembered I the word of the Lord, how he said, John indeed baptized with water; but ye shall be baptized with the Holy Spirit" (Acts 11:15-16).

In this statement Peter indicated two things: Jesus' promise concerning Spirit baptism was fulfilled when the Spirit fell on the Jewish believers at Pentecost; and the baptism with the Spirit on Pentecost took place when something new began. The word Peter used for *beginning* "Denotes beginning in the exact sense, i.e., 'the place in a temporal sequence at which something new, which is also finite, commences.' "[5]

Since the new thing began on Pentecost when the baptism with the Spirit took place, and since (as noted earlier) Spirit baptism was necessary for the formation of the Church, it would appear that Peter was indicating that the Church was the new thing that began on Pentecost.

The third line of evidence for the Church beginning in Acts 2 is Paul's teaching concerning "the mystery." Concerning the meaning of the term *mystery*, Arndt and Gingrich said,

> Our lit. uses it to mean the secret thoughts, plans, and dispensations of God which are hidden fr. the human reason, as well as fr. all other comprehension below the divine level, and hence must be

revealed to those for whom they are intended"
6 ("lit." means *literature*; "fr." means *from*).

In line with this meaning, Paul used the term *mystery* to refer to a body of divine knowledge which was kept completely hidden from man in ages past (Rom. 16:25; 1 Cor. 2:7-8; Eph. 3:4-5, 9: Col. 1:26), which man could never have discovered through the use of his senses or reason (1 Cor. 2:9), and which God has now revealed to man (Rom. 16:25-26; 1 Cor. 2:10; Eph. 3:3-5; Col. 1:26-27).

The specific body of divine knowledge which Paul called "the mystery" in Ephesians 3 was that there would be a period of time in which believing Gentiles would be equal heirs of God's blessings, equal members of the same body, and equal partakers of God's promise in Christ with believing Jews (v. 6). In Ephesians 2:11-19 Paul made it clear that Gentiles did not have these privileges before the death of Christ.

Several things should be noted concerning the Ephesians 3 *mystery*. First, it contained knowledge to the effect that there would be a period of time when believing Jews and Gentiles would be united together as equals in one body. Second, in the passage which is parallel to Ephesians 3 Paul indicated that this body, which is related to the mystery, is the Church (Col. 1:18, 24-27). Thus, in Ephesians 3 Paul was saying that the mystery contained knowledge to the effect that there would be a period of time when there would be a body called the Church existing in the world. Third, Paul made it clear that this knowledge concerning the Church had been known by God from eternity past. He said that it has been hid in God "from the beginning of the ages" (literally, "from the ages," Eph. 3:9) and that the Church had been part of God's eternal purpose (Eph. 3:11). Fourth, Paul declared that this knowledge concerning the Church had been kept hidden from man in past ages (Eph. 3:4-5, 9).

Fifth, Paul asserted that God did not reveal this knowledge concerning the Church until the time of the apostles and New Testament prophets (Eph. 3:3-5). In Colossians 1:26 he talked about "the mystery which hath been hidden from ages and from generations, but now is made manifest to his saints." Paul's use of the word *now* indicated that knowledge concerning the existence of the body called the Church was not revealed to man until Paul's lifetime.

Sixth, in Ephesians 3:8-10 Paul stated that one of the purposes of God's revealing the mystery concerning the Church during the time of the apostles and prophets was "To the intent that now, unto the principalities and powers in heavenly places, might be known by the church the manifold wisdom of God." This statement of purpose indicates that there were certain aspects of God's wisdom which were totally unknown to the angels before the Church came into existence. Nothing prior to the Church had required the use of these facets of God's wisdom. The formation of the Church demanded the exercise and, therefore, the display of aspects of divine wisdom which God never before had operated or revealed because only this unique wisdom could bring about the peaceful, equal union of such confirmed, implacable enemies as Jews and Gentiles into one body.

Once again Paul used the word *now,* indicating that God intended to wait until the time of the apostles and New Testament prophets to reveal to the angels the facets of His wisdom which the formation of the Church demanded. In Ephesians 3:11 Paul stated that God's intention to wait until that time to reveal these aspects of His wisdom was part of His eternal purpose.

Following is a summary of Paul's teaching concerning the mystery in Ephesians 3. As part of His eternal purpose for history, God in eternity past determined that there would be a time in history in which He would bring together believing Jews and Gentiles as equals to form one body, the Church. Since this was His own plan, God knew about it all along, but He kept this knowledge about the Church completely hidden in Himself and from man throughout many ages of time. Man could not discover this knowledge about the Church on his own. God intentionally waited until the time of the apostles and New Testament prophets to reveal to man knowledge concerning the Church and to reveal to angels the facets of His wisdom which the formation of the Church required to be exercised.

This teaching of Paul concerning the Ephesians 3 mystery leads to several conclusions. First, man knew nothing about the Church until the time of the apostles and New Testament prophets. Second, the Church did not exist before that time. If the Church had existed before the time of the apostles and New Testament prophets, then certainly man would have known about it before then.

Third, the Old Testament contained no revelation concerning the Church. The Old Testament did contain revelation to the effect that Gentiles would experience great salvation in the future, but revelation concerning salvation and revelation concerning the Church are not the same because salvation and the Church are not the same. Just as a ticket, which is necessary to enter a sports stadium, is not the same thing as the stadium, so salvation, which is necessary to enter the Church, is not the same thing as the Church. Although the Old Testament contained revelation concerning the salvation of Gentiles, nowhere did it contain revelation to the effect that there would be a time when saved Gentiles would be united with saved Jews as equals in one body.

Fourth, the Church was not formed until the time of the apostles and New Testament prophets. Had the Church been formed earlier, the angels would have known about those aspects of God's wisdom earlier.

The fourth line of evidence concerning when the Church began is that the Church could not exist until after the death of Christ. In Ephesians 2:13-16 Paul made statements that Gentiles, who used to be far off, now have been brought near "by the the blood of Christ" (v. 13); that Jesus himself is the peace between Jew and Gentile (v. 14); that He is the one who has made Jew and Gentile one, has broken down the dividing wall between them, has abolished the enmity "in his flesh," has made *one new man* of Jew and Gentile "in himself," and has reconciled both Jew and Gentile unto God *in one body* "by the cross" (vv. 14-16).

Several things should be noted concerning these statements. First, they clearly indicate that the uniting of Jew and Gentile together as equals to form one new man, one body, was the result of Jesus shedding His blood or dying on the cross. Second, a comparison of these statements with Paul's statements in Ephesians 3:6 and Colossians 1:18, 24 makes it obvious that the one body of Ephesians 2:16 is the Church. Third, the Church was formed as the result of Jesus' death.

Fourth, in the statements of Ephesians 2:13-16 Paul was emphasizing the situation of Gentiles after the death of Christ in contrast with their situation before His death (vv. 11-12). One aspect of the contrast was that before the death of Christ, the Gentiles were alienated from the Jews; but after Christ's death, Gentiles were united with Jews in one body. Paul's use of the word *now* (v. 13) indicated that this radical change of situation had taken place during his lifetime. This means that the one body, the Church, was not formed until Paul's lifetime after Christ's death.

Fifth, Paul described the union of Jew and Gentile as "one new man" (v. 15). The word which is translated *new* has the following meanings: "what is new and distinctive as compared with other things," "what is new in nature, different from the usual," and "new in kind."[7] It would appear, then, that this union of Jew and Gentile formed a new body which was different in nature and kind from anything that had ever existed before. It was not a continuation of something which already had been in existence and which was essentially the same in nature.

Since the uniting of Jew and Gentile together as equals to form one body was the result of Christ's death, since that body was formed only after Christ's death, since that body was new and different in nature and kind from anything that had ever existed before, and since that one body is the Church, then the Church did not and could not exist until after the death of Christ.

A statement which Paul made to the Ephesian elders also leads to the conclusion that the Church could not have existed until after Christ's death. In that statement Paul referred to "the church of God, which he hath purchased with his own blood" (Acts 20:28). The word which is translated *purchased* means "acquire, obtain, gain for oneself."[8] Paul, therefore, was declaring that Jesus acquired or obtained the Church through His death. The implication is that Jesus did not have the Church before He shed His blood.

The fifth line of evidence concerning the time when the Church began is that the Church could not exist before the apostles and New Testament prophets. In Ephesians 2:11-16 Paul taught that God had started to do something new. In past ages the Gentiles had been alienated from the Jews and had been "without God in the world" (v. 12), but during Paul's lifetime God started to bring Gentiles and Jews together as equals to form "one new man" (v. 15), "one body" (v. 16).

In Ephesians 2:19-22 Paul continued his teaching concerning this new work of God through the use of a metaphor — the metaphor of a building. He declared that Gentiles are no longer strangers and aliens but are members of the "household of God" (v. 19). In 1 Timothy 3:15 Paul clearly stated that the household of God is the Church; therefore, in Ephesians 2:19 he was teaching that Gentiles are members of the Church.

Paul began to use the metaphor of a building by asserting that the members of the Church "are built upon the foundation of the apostles and prophets" (v. 20). Several things should be noted concerning this assertion. First, since the Church consists of its members, and since the members are built upon the foundation of the apostles and prophets, then Paul was indicating that the Church itself is built upon the foundation of the apostles and prophets. Second, continuing his use of the metaphor of a building, Paul pointed out that just as a building has a foundation and superstructure, so the Church has a foundation and superstructure. The Church's foundation consists of the apostles and prophets, and its superstructure consists of the other Church saints. Third, the prophets who, together with the apostles, make up the foundation of the Church are New Testament prophets, not Old Testament prophets. The context indicates that this is so, for in Ephesians 3:5, where Paul referred to the apostles and prophets again, he said, "as it is now revealed unto his holy apostles and prophets." Through the use of the word *now*, Paul made it clear that the prophets to whom he referred were living during his lifetime and that of other apostles.

Fourth, since a building cannot be built without a foundation, and since the Church's foundation consists of the apostles and New Testament prophets, then the Church could not have been built before the time of the apostles and New Testament prophets. According to Arndt and Gingrich, the word which Paul used for *foundation* has the meaning "of the indispensable prerequisites for someth. to come into being" in Ephesians 2:20.[9] In other words, the Church could not come into being apart from the apostles and New Testament prophets.

The sixth line of evidence for when the Church began is Jesus' promise in Matthew 16:18, "I will build my church." The verb which is translated *will build* is future tense and indicative mood in the text, and "the future indicative expresses anticipation of an event in future time."[10]

The implication of Jesus' statement is that the Church was not in existence when He said this. The Church would be something new which He would build in the future. Thus, Michel stated that the verb *will build* in Matthew 16:18 "denotes an eschatalogical act of Christ, a new authorisation by God. The Messiah will build...the new community."[11]

Prior to His Matthew 16:18 statement, Jesus had been presenting Himself to Israel as its Messiah, the One who would set up the promised Theocratic Kingdom of God. He had claimed to be the Messiah (Jn. 10:24-25); through His miracles He had given Israel a foretaste of the miraculous powers by which Messiah would usher in the Theocratic Kingdom (Lk. 7:19-22; Jn. 10:25, 12:37; 20:30-31; Acts 2:22; Heb. 6:5); He had preached the gospel of the Kingdom: "Repent; for the kingdom of heaven is at hand" (Mt. 4:17, 23; 9:35); and He had commissioned His apostles to preach the gospel of the Kingdom and to perform the miracles associated with the Kingdom only to the people of Israel (Mt. 10:1-8).

In spite of Jesus' claim to be the Messiah who would set up the Theocratic Kingdom, and in spite of the foretaste of miraculous kingdom powers which demonstrated the truthfulness of His claim, Israel was determined to reject Him and His claim (Jn. 12:37-41). This determination had become obvious before Jesus' Matthew 16 declaration that He would build His Church. In Matthew 12 the religious leaders of Israel had begun to plot His death and to assert that Satan was the source of His miraculous powers. In Matthew 16 the apostles reported the reaction of the people to Jesus (vv. 13-14). The Jews were saying that He was John the Baptist, Elijah, Jeremiah, or one of the prophets, but they were not acclaiming Him to be the Messiah.

In light of Israel's obvious determination, in Matthew 16 Jesus began to give His apostles several indications to the effect that things would change significantly for Him and His ministry. One indication was Jesus' shocking declaration of His death and resurrection (v. 21). Matthew's words, "From that time forth began Jesus to show unto his disciples, how he must...be killed, and be raised again the third day," reveal the fact that Jesus had never clearly declared His death and resurrection to the apostles prior to this time. Peter's strong negative reaction to Jesus' declaration (v. 22) indicated that this was a shocking new concept to the apostles and that the gospel of the Kingdom which they had been proclaiming for some time did not include the ideas of Jesus' death, burial, and resurrection. Thus, through this shocking declaration Jesus was indicating that instead of Israel's accepting Him as its Messiah, it would reject Him by having Him put to death.

Another indication of coming change given by Jesus in Matthew 16 was His charge to the apostles "that they should tell no man" that He was the Messiah (v. 20). Earlier they had proclaimed Him to be the Messiah (Jn. 1:41), but now they were forbidden to do so.

A third indication of change for Jesus and His ministry was His Matthew 16:18 declaration. Since Israel would reject Him as the Messiah who set up the Theocratic Kingdom, He would not establish that Kingdom in the near future.

Instead, He would do something different — He would build a new *ekklesia*, the Church. There were other *ekklesias* or assemblies in the ancient world, such as the *ekklesia* of Israel in the wilderness during its exodus (Acts 7:38) and the *ekklesias* of citizens of cities when they gathered together for public meetings (Acts 19:32, 39, 41), but Jesus emphasized the fact that the *ekklesia* which He would build would be uniquely related to Him ("my church"). The Israel of Jesus' generation refused to be associated with Him; therefore, He would build a new assembly of people which would acknowledge and belong to Him. Later, the Apostle Paul emphasized the unique relationship of the Church to Christ through the use of the relationships between the body and head (Eph. 1:22-23; 4:15-16; 5:23; Col. 1:18; 2:19) and bride and bridegroom (Rom. 7:1-4; 2 Cor. 11:2; Eph. 5:22-23).

The seventh line of evidence concerning when the Church began is that the Church could not exist until after Christ's ascension. Two things indicate that this is so. First, in Ephesians 1:20-23 Paul taught that God gave Christ the position of Head to the Church in conjunction with Christ's being seated at God's right hand after His ascension to Heaven. This means that Christ was not Head to the Church until after His ascension. In Ephesians 4:15-16 and Colossians 2:19 Paul also taught that the Church is dependent upon Christ as its Head for its growth and development. Just as the human body cannot live, function, or develop without its head, so the body of Christ, the Church, cannot live, function, or develop without Christ as its Head. In light of these facts, the Church could not have existed until after Christ's ascension.

Second, in Ephesians 4:8, 11-12 Paul indicated that in conjunction with His ascension to Heaven Christ gave spiritual gifts to human beings so that the body of Christ, the Church, could be built. Through this teaching Paul implied that the Church could not be built apart from these spiritual gifts, and, therefore, the Church could not have existed before His ascension.

Evidence That Israel And The Church Are Not The Same

In the previous chapter it was noted that Covenant Theology proposes that the Church is the continuing covenanted community of God's people throughout history. It consists of all people who have had the Covenant of Grace relationship with God regardless of the period of history in which they have lived. Thus, the Church is the same in essence throughout history.

Covenant Theology further asserts that Israel was the major people of God in Old Testament times because God entered into Mosaic Covenant relationship with that nation, and the Mosaic Covenant relationship was one aspect of the Covenant of Grace relationship.

Covenant Theology also teaches that the New Testament Church is the people of God today because God entered into the New Covenant relationship with the New Testament Church, and the New Covenant relationship is also an aspect of the Covenant of Grace relationship.

These concepts have led Covenant Theology to the following logical conclusions: Since the Church consists of all people who have had the Covenant of Grace relationship with God regardless of when they have lived, and since both Old Testament Israel and the New Testament Church have had the Covenant of Grace relationship with God, then the Church consists of both Old Testament Israel and the New Testament Church, which are essentially the same.

In contrast with this view, there are several lines of evidence to the effect that Old Testament Israel and the New Testament

Church are not essentially the same. First, Old Testament Israel was a nation in the technical sense of that term, but the New Testament Church is not a nation in the technical sense. Several factors illustrate this distinctive. Old Testament Israel had a national language, but the New Testament Church is comprised of people with many different languages. Old Testament Israel was an earthly, political state with an earthly capital city, an earthly political government, and political rulers, but the New Testament Church does not have an earthly capital city, an earthly political government, or political rulers. In His Mosaic Covenant relationship with Israel, God established and regulated that nation's earthly, political government, but in His New Covenant relationship with the New Testament Church, God does not establish an earthly, political government for the Church. Old Testament Israel had a common, national tradition and history, but the New Testament Church is comprised of people from many different national traditions and histories. Old Testament Israel had a national army with which to fight military battles against other nations, but the New Testament Church does not have such an army.

Second, in spite of the fact that Old Testament Israel was the people of God through its Mosaic Covenant relationship with Him, it rejected Christ, just as God had forewarned the nation that it would (Isa. 53; Jn. 1:11; 12:37-41). By contrast, the New Testament Church received Christ.

A third evidence that Old Testament Israel and the New Testament Church are not the same is that Old Testament Israel was the original persecutor of the New Testament Church.

Fourth, as long as a Gentile remained a Gentile, he was excluded from membership in Old Testament Israel (Eph. 2:11-12). In order to become a member, he had to become an Israelite through circumcision and placement under the Law. In other words, he had to enter fully into Israel's Mosaic

Covenant relationship with God. By contrast, a Gentile can be in full, equal membership in the New Testament Church as a Gentile. He does not have to become an Israelite in order to enter that membership (Eph. 2:13-16; 3:1-6). The Holy Spirit led the early leaders of the New Testament Church to recognize this distinction which God had made between Old Testament Israel and the New Testament Church (Acts 15:1-29).

Fifth, Old Testament Israel had both believers and unbelievers in full Mosaic Covenant relationship with God. When God established the Mosaic Covenant with Israel, He established it fully with the entire membership of that nation, saved and unsaved alike. All the Israelites were subject to the regulations of the covenant regardless of their inner spiritual state. Regeneration was not required of those at Mount Sinai in order to enter the Mosaic Covenant relationship with God, and future generations of Israelites entered that covenant relationship by virtue of their physical birth to Israelite parents, not by virtue of a spiritual birth. The unsaved members of Old Testament Israel were as much the Mosaic Covenant people of God as were the saved members, and Old Testament Israel's membership consisted of unsaved people as well as the saved.

By contrast, the New Testament Church (not organized Christendom but the true body of Christ which is formed by Spirit baptism) consists only of saved or regenerated members. Two things indicate that this is so. First, Luke declared that the Lord was adding to the Church *those who were being saved* (Acts 2:47). In addition, it is Spirit baptism which forms the Church, and Spirit baptism happens only to the saved. On the Day of Pentecost, only the saved Jews were baptized with the Spirit; the unsaved Jews were not (Acts 2). In spite of the fact that Cornelius was a God-fearing

Gentile (Acts 10:1-2), he was not baptized with the Spirit until he was saved (Acts 10:44-47; 11:13-18). Since Spirit baptism happens only to the saved, and since it is Spirit baptism which forms the Church, the Church has only saved people in its membership.

Sixth, the Scriptures never called the saved Jews of Old Testament Israel *the Church of God* in contrast with the unsaved Jews of Old Testament Israel, but the Scriptures did call the saved Jews (and the saved Gentiles) of the New Testament Church *the Church of God* in contrast with the unsaved Jews (and the unsaved Gentiles) of the New Testament era (1 Cor. 10:32). The fact that the Scriptures applied the term *the Church of God* to the saved Jews of the New Testament Church but did not apply it to the saved Jews of Old Testament Israel implies three things: There is a distinction between the saved Jews of the New Testament Church and the saved Jews of Old Testament Israel; the term *the Church of God* can be applied legitimately only to the New Testament Church but not to Old Testament Israel; and Old Testament Israel and the New Testament Church are not essentially the same.

Seventh, in Romans 11 the Apostle Paul presented the following teaching: As the covenant people of God, Old Testament Israel was in the place of God's blessing. Because Old Testament Israel rejected Christ through unbelief, God removed it temporarily from the place of His blessing. During the time that Israel is removed, God has placed the New Testament Church into the place of blessing. Thus, the Church is in the place of God's blessing while Israel is out of it. God will restore Israel to the place of His blessing when Israel receives Christ at His Second Coming. In light of this teaching, the following conclusion can be drawn: Since Israel is out of the place of God's blessing while the Church is in it, Israel and the Church are not the same.[12]

SIXTEEN

THE RELATIONSHIP OF THE CHRISTIAN TO LAW AND GRACE

The Problem Stated

Covenant Theology and Dispensational Theology disagree concerning the relationship of the Christian to the Mosaic Law. Covenant Theology advocates the position that Christians today are not under the civil and ceremonial aspects of the Mosaic Law, but they are under the moral aspect (the Ten Commandments) of the Law. Failure to be under the moral aspect of the Mosaic Law is to be lawless. The moral aspect of the Law presents the eternal, moral absolutes of God, which are unchangeable. If a person is not under the moral aspect of the Mosaic Law, that person is unrelated to the eternal, unchangeable, moral absolutes of God. Thus, there are only two alternatives open to the Christian — either be under the moral aspect of the Mosaic Law or be lawless.

In contrast with the Covenant Theology view, Dispensational Theology holds the position that Christians today are not under any aspect of the Mosaic Law, even the moral aspect. It should be noted that although the Mosaic Law had three aspects (civil, ceremonial, and moral), it functioned as an indivisible unit. Thus, to place oneself under one aspect of the Mosaic Law is to obligate oneself to be under the entire Law. If a person is under the moral aspect of the Law, he is required to keep all the civil and ceremonial regulations as well.

In addition, the fact that a person is not under the moral aspect of the Mosaic Law does not mean that he is unrelated to the eternal, unchangeable, moral absolutes of God. Although the Mosaic Law did present the eternal, unchangeable, moral absolutes of God, it was only one way of God's administering His moral absolutes to one group of people (the nation of Israel) during one period of history (from God's meeting with Israel at Mount Sinai to the cross of Jesus Christ) [Dt. 4:8-14; 5:1-22; Gal. 3:19, 23-25].

Since God's moral absolutes are eternal, they have been in effect throughout all of history; thus they were in effect before God instituted the Mosaic Law at Mount Sinai. This means that prior to Mount Sinai God administered His unchangeable, moral absolutes in ways other than through the Mosaic Law. It also means that God's eternal, moral absolutes can be in effect without the Mosaic Law being in effect.

In addition, it should be noted that before the Mosaic Law was instituted there were people who lived righteous lives in conformity to God's moral absolutes. Abel (Heb. 11:4), Enoch (Gen. 5:22, 24; Heb. 11:5), Noah (Gen. 6:9; Ezek. 14:14, 20), and Job (Job 1:8; 2:3; Ezek. 14:14, 20) are examples of such people. It is interesting to note that God placed Noah and Job (who lived without the Mosaic Law) in the same category of righteousness as Daniel (who lived under the Mosaic Law) [Ezek. 14:14, 20]. The fact that some people lived righteous lives in conformity to God's moral absolutes before the Mosaic Law was instituted indicates two things: People can be related to the eternal, unchangeable, moral absolutes of God without being under the moral aspect of the Mosaic Law; and it is possible for a person to be free from the moral aspect of the Mosaic Law without being lawless.

Prior to Mount Sinai, God administered His moral absolutes over all of mankind in ways other than through the Mosaic

Law. From Mount Sinai to the cross of Jesus Christ, He administered His moral absolutes over Israel through the Mosaic Law. Since the time of the cross, God has been administering His eternal absolutes over all of mankind in a way which is different from and superior to the Mosaic Law. The moral absolutes have not changed, but the way of God's administering those absolutes has changed. For example, idolatry and adultery have been just as wrong in God's sight since the time of the cross as they were when the Mosaic Law was in effect, but since the cross God has not required the death penalty for these sins (1 Cor. 6:9-11) as He did when the Mosaic Law was in effect (Ex. 22:20; Lev. 20:10). The new, superior way of God's administering His moral absolutes is called *grace*.

In light of what has been seen, the Dispensational position prompts two significant conclusions: Freedom from the moral aspect of the Mosaic Law does not involve freedom from the eternal, unchangeable, moral absolutes of God. It only involves freedom from one way of God's administering His absolutes — namely, through the Mosaic Law. Also, there are more than two alternatives open to the Christian — either be under the moral aspect of the Mosaic Law or be lawless. There is a third alternative — if one is under God's *grace* in administering His eternal, unchangeable, moral absolutes, one will not be lawless.

Evidence That The Mosaic Law Was An Indivisible Unit

Dispensational Theology bases its belief concerning the indivisible nature of the Mosaic Law upon three biblical passages. In Galatians 3:10 Paul wrote, "For as many as are of the works of the law are under the curse; for it is written, Cursed is everyone that continueth not in all things which are written in the book of the law, to do them." One of the implications of this statement is that the person who attempted to keep the Mosaic Law was required to keep *every* aspect of the Law perfectly and continuously. In other words, the Mosaic Law was an indivisible unit. The keeping of one part of it obligated a person to keep every part of it.

In Galatians 5:3 Paul stated, "For I testify again to every man that is circumcised, that he is a debtor to do the whole law." Circumcision was one part of the ceremonial aspect of the Mosaic Law. Paul was asserting that submission to only one part of the ceremonial aspect of the Law obligated a person to keep every aspect of the Law. Once again he was emphasizing the indivisible nature of the Law.

James declared, "For whosoever shall keep the whole law, and yet offend in one point, he is guilty of all" (Jas. 2:10). James was asserting that the breaking of only one part of the Mosaic Law made a person guilty of breaking the entire Law. The only way this could be true was if the Mosaic Law were an indivisible unit.

The fact that the Mosaic Law was indivisible by nature has a strong implication concerning the relationship of the Christian to the Mosaic Law. The implication is that since the Mosaic Law was indivisible by nature, the Christian who places himself under its moral aspect obligates himself to keep every aspect of the Law (the civil, ceremonial, and moral).

Evidence That Christians Are Not Under The Mosaic Law

Several Scriptures indicate that Christians are not under the Mosaic Law. Twice in Romans 6:14-15 Paul declared that Christians (including himself) are not under law but under grace. In Romans 7:4 Paul asserted that Christians have become dead to the Law through Christ's physical death. In the context of this statement, Paul's point was that the Christian's death to the Mosaic Law freed him from obligation to it. Again in Romans 7:6 Paul stated that the Christian's death to the Mosaic Law delivered him from that Law. The word translated *delivered* meant "to take from the sphere of operation."[1] The Christian, therefore, has been removed from the Mosaic Law's sphere of operation. He further taught that this removal results in the Christian's serving God in the newness of the Spirit, not in the oldness of the Mosaic Law. Thus, the Christian serves God in a sphere of administration of His absolutes which is different from the Mosaic Law.

In Galatians 2:19 Paul declared that he died to the Law with the purpose that he might live to God. The implication is that a believer must be separated from a relationship with the Mosaic Law in order to experience true spiritual life. In Galatians 3:19 he indicated that the Mosaic Law was intended to be temporary. It was to be in effect only until the first coming of Jesus Christ, Abraham's seed. Paul enlarged this concept of the temporary nature of the Law by teaching that the Law functioned as a pedagogue (a moral restrainer or disciplinarian) only until the faith, which came through Jesus Christ's earthly ministry, arrived. Once that faith arrived, believers were not under the pedagogue (the Law) [Gal. 3:23-25].

In Galatians 5:18 Paul wrote that the person who is led by (controlled by) the Holy Spirit is not under the Law. In Romans 8:14 Paul indicated that it is the Christian who is led by the Spirit. Thus, through his Galatians 5:18 statement Paul was asserting that the Christian is not under the Law. Then he stated that there is no law against the fruit of the Spirit (which is produced by the Spirit in a believer's life) [Gal. 5:22-23]. Paul's point in these statements was that the Holy Spirit produces righteous fruit in the Christian. Since this fruit is righteous by nature, and since the Mosaic Law was ordained to restrain unrighteousness (lawlessness) [Gal. 3:19], it isn't necessary to have the Mosaic Law in effect to oppose the righteous fruit of the Spirit in the life of a Christian. Thus, the Christian is not under the Mosaic Law.

Paul declared that the Mosaic Law was abolished by Jesus Christ through His physical death on the cross (Eph. 2:15-16). The word translated *abolished* meant "to put out of business" or "to dissolve business relationships."[2] The idea behind this declaration is that from the time God met with Israel at Mount Sinai to the time of Christ's death on the cross, God employed the Mosaic Law as His way of administering His moral absolutes over Israel. But when Christ died, God stopped employing the Mosaic Law; He dissolved His relationship with it; He put the Law out of business. Thus, believers since the cross have not been under the Mosaic Law even as a moral rule of life.

According to the writer of Hebrews, the Old Testament Scriptures indicated that eventually the Aaronic priesthood would be replaced by a priest after the order of Melchizedek (Heb. 7). Thus, the Old Testament implied that the Aaronic priesthood was temporary. On that basis the writer of Hebrews carried his teaching a step further by declaring, "For the priesthood being changed, there is made of necessity a change also of the law" (Heb. 7:12). F. F. Bruce stated that the word translated *change* in this statement "implies not merely change but abrogation."[3] Thus, the writer of Hebrews was indicating that when Jesus Christ abolished the Aaronic priesthood through the establishment of His Melchizedekian priestly ministry, the Mosaic Law which established the Aaronic priesthood was also abolished.

Concerning this teaching by the writer of Hebrews, F. F. Bruce declared,

Nor is it only the Aaronic priesthood which must be superseded. That priesthood was instituted under the Mosaic law, and was so integral to it that a change in the priesthood carries with it inevitably a change in the law. If the Aaronic priesthood was instituted for a temporary purpose, to be brought to an end when the age of fulfillment dawned, the same must be true of the law under which that priesthood was introduced. So by his own independent line of argument our author reaches the same conclusion as Paul: the law was a temporary provision, "our tutor to bring us unto Christ...but now that faith is come, we are no longer under a tutor" (Gal. 3:24f)...If we like, we may say that Paul has the moral law mainly in mind, whereas the author of Hebrews is concerned more with the ceremonial law...although the distinction between the moral and ceremonial law is one drawn by Christian theologians, not by those who accepted the whole law as the will of God, nor yet by the New Testament writers. But in principle Paul and our author are agreed that the law was a temporary dispensation of God, valid only until Christ came to inaugurate the age of perfection.[4]

Since Jesus abolished the Mosaic Law when He abolished the Aaronic priesthood, it can be concluded that Christians today are not under the Mosaic Law.

This chapter has presented evidence for two conclusions. First, the Mosaic Law is an indivisible unit. Thus, if a person places himself under the moral aspect of the Mosaic Law, he obligates himself to keep the entire Law (including the civil and ceremonial aspects). Second, the Christian is not under any aspect of the Mosaic Law.

The next chapter will explore the fact that Christ established grace as the new way of God administering His eternal, unchangeable, moral absolutes. It will also examine the manner in which God administers His moral absolutes through grace.

SEVENTEEN

THE GRACE ADMINISTRATION OF GOD'S MORAL ABSOLUTES

INTRODUCTION

Evidence That Christ Established Grace As The New Way of God's Administering His Moral Absolutes

S everal New Testament passages indicate that Jesus Christ, through His ministry during His first coming, established grace as the new way of God's administering His moral absolutes.

The Apostle John wrote, "For the law was given by Moses, but grace and truth came by Jesus Christ" (Jn. 1:17). Several observations should be made concerning John's statement. First, John was teaching that during His first coming Jesus brought into being a new form of divine grace which had not existed in Old Testament times. Two things indicate that this was the apostle's teaching. First, in John's statement "grace and truth came by Jesus Christ," the verb which is translated *came* means "come to be, become, originate."[1] Thus, John was saying that some form of grace came into being or originated through Jesus Christ during His first coming which did not exist prior to that time.

Second, John also declared that of Jesus' "fullness have all we received, and grace for grace" (Jn. 1:16). The expression *grace for grace* means "grace after or upon grace (i.e., grace pours forth in ever new streams)."[2] Again the implication seems to be that during His first coming, Jesus enlarged grace by adding a new form of it to all the forms of grace which had already existed during Old Testament times.

A second observation concerning the John 1:17 statement is that the new form of grace to which John referred cannot be that form which brings salvation from the penalty of sin. At least two things indicate that this is so. First, as noted in the first observation, the new form of grace which came into being during Jesus' first coming did *not* exist in Old Testament times. In Romans 4:1-16 Paul taught that both Abraham (who lived before the Mosaic Law was given) and David (who lived under the Law) were justified from the penalty of sin by grace.

Second, John's statement in John 1:17 seems to imply that the new form of grace which originated through Jesus was intended to serve as the contrasting replacement of the Law which God gave through Moses. In other words, the new form of grace was to have the same basic function as the Law, but it was to fulfill that function in a significantly different way. In light of this, it is important to note that the Mosaic Law never functioned as a means of eternal salvation. No person has ever been justified through the Law (Rom. 3:28; Gal. 2:16, 21; 3:11). In fact, instead of saving people, the Law was a ministry of condemnation, death, and wrath (2 Cor. 3:7, 9; Rom. 4:15) to those who were under it.

Although the Mosaic Law was never a means of eternal salvation, it did function as a new, particular way of God's administering His eternal, moral absolutes.

It would appear that John was teaching the following in John 1:17: God established the Mosaic Law as a way of administering His eternal, moral absolutes through Moses, but Jesus Christ established grace as the new way of God's administering His moral absolutes.

A second passage which indicates this fact is Romans 6:14, where Paul declared to Christians, "For sin shall not have dominion over you; for ye are not under the law but under grace." Several things should be noted concerning Paul's statement. First, he clearly asserted that the Christian is not under the Law.

Second, Paul implied that the form of grace which he had in mind had the same function as the Law. He did this by making *law* and *grace* the objects of the same preposition *under*. As noted earlier, that function cannot be eternal salvation, because the Law was never a means of salvation. To be *under* law or grace meant to be subject to the "power, rule, sovereignty, command"[3] of law or grace as rules of life. It can be concluded, therefore, that Paul was referring to Law and grace as ways of God's administering His moral absolutes over human beings.

Third, Paul taught that being under the grace administration rather than the Law administration frees the Christian from mastery by the sin nature. This means that it is advantageous to be under the grace administration, which is superior to the Law administration.

Fourth, in Romans 6:15 Paul asserted that being under the grace administration does not give the Christian liberty to sin (to be lawless). Thus, it is possible for a person to be free from even the moral aspect of the Mosaic Law without being lawless, and the grace administration does not encourage a sinful lifestyle.

Fifth, in Romans 7:1, 4, where Paul explained his teaching in Romans 6:14, he indicated that Jewish Christians were set free from the Law administration of God's rule through their association with Christ's death. Paul further asserted that the ultimate purpose of this freedom was a fruitful life for God through association with the resurrected Christ. The implication seems to be that Jesus Christ, through His ministry during His first coming, ended the Law administration and established the grace administration.[4]

The third passage which indicates that Jesus established grace as the new way of God's administering His moral absolutes is Titus 2:11-14. Paul wrote,

For the grace of God that bringeth salvation hath appeared to all men, Teaching us that, denying ungodliness and worldly lusts, we should live soberly, righteously, and godly, in this present age, Looking for that blessed hope, and the glorious appearing of the great God and our Savior, Jesus Christ, Who gave himself for us that he might redeem us from all iniquity, and purify unto himself a people of his own, zealous of good works.

Paul's statement indicates several things. First, the grace of God has more than one function. One function is that of bringing eternal salvation to human beings, but another function is that of teaching Christians how to live.

Second, the way in which grace teaches Christians how to live is by functioning as a rule of life. The word translated *teaching* in Titus 2:12 "denotes the upbringing and handling of the child which is growing up to maturity and which thus needs direction, teaching, instruction, and a certain measure of compulsion in the form of discipline or even chastisement."[5] The term was used of "activity directed to the moral and spiritual nurture and training of the child, to influence conscious will and action."[6] In other words, this form of teaching does far more than just impart precepts. It governs lifestyle and molds character. Thus, when Paul referred to this teaching activity of grace, he was talking about grace functioning as a rule of life.

Third, Paul indicated that as a rule of life, grace teaches Christians to reject a godless, worldly lifestyle and to practice a godly, righteous lifestyle. Since such a godly lifestyle would have to involve conformity to God's eternal, moral absolutes, and since as a rule of life grace works to produce such a lifestyle, it would seem that this grace rule of life is an administration of God's eternal, moral absolutes.

Fourth, grace is the particular way of God's administering His moral absolutes in this present age. Paul declared that grace is teaching believers to live godly lives "in this present age" (literally, "in the now age," v.12). The fact that grace is teaching believers to live godly lives in this present age indicates that this teaching function of grace is also going on in this present age. The implication is that the grace administration of God's absolutes is distinctive to this present age.

Fifth, this grace administration of God's absolutes was established through Christ's ministry in His first coming. Paul indicated this through two things. First, in Titus 2:11 he declared, "For the grace of God...hath appeared." Many scholars are convinced that Paul used the expression *hath appeared* to refer to Christ's first coming. The English word *epiphany,* which is used frequently as a reference to Christ's first coming, is derived from Paul's word which is translated *hath appeared.* Concerning this, Kent wrote, "Our word 'epiphany' is a derivative. Thus the epiphany here referred to was Christ's first coming."[7]

Second, in Titus 2:14 Paul taught that Jesus gave Himself (through death) for the purpose of obtaining a people whose lives would be characterized by freedom from lawlessness (literal translation of the term translated *iniquity*) and by the kind of godly, righteous lifestyle which grace teaches Christians to have (v. 12). It would appear, then, that Christ's death played a key role in establishing the teaching function of grace.

Through these two things Paul indicated that Christ established grace as a way of God's administering His moral absolutes through His first coming ministry.

The Manner Of The Grace Administration Of God's Moral Absolutes

The Manner Contrasted and Described

Through the Mosaic Law, God administered His eternal, moral absolutes in an *external* manner. The moral heart of the Law was written on tablets of stone outside the people. Each new generation of Israelites came under the Law administration by virtue of physical birth to Israelite parents and external circumcision, not by virtue of an internal change. The Mosaic Law emphasized the need for an internal change, but it did not produce that change. The Law stood outside the Israelites and required conformity to the will of God, but it provided neither the will nor the power needed internally to conform. The Law inflicted external punishments, such as physical death, upon those who broke it.

By contrast, through grace God administers His eternal, moral absolutes in an *internal* manner. This manner involves a combination of two internal things. The first is a confirmed, favorable disposition toward God. This disposition consists of the law of God in the heart and has been called "the new nature" by many theologians. It is placed in the heart (the inner control center of the Christian) through the regenerating work of the Holy Spirit. The second internal thing is the indwelling Holy Spirit, who takes permanent residence inside the body of the Christian at the moment of salvation.

The Manner Promised

Through Old Testament prophets, God promised both things which, when combined, constitute the manner of the grace administration of God's moral absolutes. For example, in Jeremiah 31:31-34 God pledged to Israel a future New Covenant which would be different from the Mosaic Law Covenant. God promised that in contrast with the Mosaic

Law Covenant, which had the law of God written on tablets of stone in the form of external precepts, the New Covenant would have the law of God written within human hearts in the form of an internal, favorable disposition toward God. Concerning this promise, Gray wrote that God was pledging to give the Israelites "a right disposition."[8] Habel said, "The new covenant, however, will not have an external set of laws, no decalog inscribed in stone, but an innate sensitivity to the will of God. The law will be part of man's nature."[9] Bennett declared, "Jehovah no longer seeks to ensure their fidelity by an external law, with its alternate threats and promises: He will rather control the inner life by His grace."[10]

God also promised that all those who would have His law written in their hearts would know Him in a unique sense as a result of His forgiving and forgetting their sins (Jer. 31:34). This cannot be referring to a general, intellectual knowledge of God's existence and power because even unsaved Jews whose sins were not forgiven and forgotten possessed such general knowledge. Instead, it refers to the experiential knowledge of God which comes through the regenerating work of the Holy Spirit. Keil wrote,

> The knowledge of Jahweh, of which the prophet speaks, is not the theoretic knowledge which is imparted and acquired by means of religious instruction; it is rather knowledge of divine grace based upon the inward experience of the heart, which knowledge the Holy Spirit works in the heart.[11]

Since it would be those who would have God's law in their hearts who would possess this unique knowledge of God, and since that knowledge would come through the regenerating work of the Holy Spirit, it would appear that the law in the heart (the favorable disposition toward God) also would come through regeneration. Calvin recognized this to be so, for he declared that the promise of God's law in the heart deals with "the grace of regeneration."[12]

A second key Old Testament passage which contained promises related to the grace administration of God's moral absolutes is Ezekiel 36:25-27. There God promises to place both a new human spirit (v. 26) and His Spirit (the Holy Spirit) [v. 27] within Israelites in the future. Concerning the promise of a new human spirit, Ellison stated that the term *spirit* in verse 26 "tends to mean his dominant disposition."[13] Snaith declared that the term was used "to denote the dominant impulse or disposition of an individual."[14] The promise of the new human spirit in Ezekiel 36:26 was exactly parallel with the promise of the law of God in the heart in Jeremiah 31:33. Both referred to the same favorable disposition toward God.

In addition to the new, favorable disposition, God promised the indwelling of His Holy Spirit (Ezek. 36:27). This would provide the Israelites with a continual source of divine power. Snaith stated,

> The idea of a more-than-human power runs through the whole of the use of the phrase [Spirit of the Lord]. As a result of this special endowment of divine power men are able to do that which, in the ordinary way and relying upon purely human resources, they are quite unable to do.[15]

As a result of God's placing both the new, favorable disposition and the Holy Spirit inside future Israelites, they would be obedient to His will (Ezek. 36:27). The favorable disposition would give the regenerate Israelite "the desire and urge to do God's will,"[16] and the Holy Spirit would give him the power to do God's will.

The Manner Applied to Church Saints

The promises of Jeremiah 31:31-34 and Ezekiel 36:25-27 were specifically to Israel. They were to be fulfilled as part of God's future New Covenant relationship with the nation. However, as noted in an earlier treatment of the New Covenant, although the Church is not Israel and does not partake of the material and national promises of the New Covenant, it does partake of the spiritual promises. Since the law of God in the heart (the favorable disposition) and the indwelling Holy Spirit were part of the spiritual promises of the New Covenant, one would expect the New Testament to indicate that Church saints have both of these factors of the grace administration of God's moral absolutes.

Several things in the New Testament demonstrate that Church saints have the law of God in the heart. First, in Titus 3:5 Paul taught that Church saints have been regenerated, and, as noted in Jeremiah 31, it is the regenerating work of the Holy Spirit which places the law of God in the heart. Second, in 2 Corinthians 3:3 Paul declared that Christ wrote something through the Holy Spirit in the hearts of Church saints. He contrasted this writing in hearts with the writing on tablets of stone of the Mosaic Law Covenant (vv. 3, 7). Paul associated the writing in hearts with New Covenant ministry (v. 6). It seems apparent that Paul was drawing the same contrast between the Mosaic Law Covenant and the New Covenant as was drawn by Jeremiah 31. Since the contrast is the same, the writing in human hearts of 2 Corinthians 3 must be the same thing as the law of God written in the heart of Jeremiah 31. Thus, Paul was teaching that through the Holy Spirit Christ wrote the law of God in the hearts of Church saints.

Third, as a Church saint Paul indicated that something within him gave him a deep-seated moral sympathy with what God declares to be right (Rom. 7:22) and prompted him to will to do what God says is right (Rom. 7:18). Since, as noted in the treatment of Ezekiel 36, this was the same kind of activity which was to be performed by the new human spirit or disposition, it would appear that Paul possessed the new, favorable disposition toward God (the law of God in the heart).

Fourth, Peter told Church saints that they are partakers of God's nature (2 Pet. 1:4). Peter did not mean that Church saints partake of omnipresence, omniscience, omnipotence, or the other attributes of God's nature which determine that He is deity. Man never partakes of God's nature in that sense because man can never become deity. Instead, Peter meant that Church saints partake of God's holy disposition; they have received a disposition which is an expression of God's holy nature. This is indicated by the context (vv. 3, 5) which is concerned with what produces a godly, moral life. Demarest wrote, " 'Nature,' then, as here used by the apostle, cannot mean essence or substance, but disposition, moral qualities. And *to become partakers of a divine nature*, means to become partakers of a disposition like that of God."[17]

A number of things in the New Testament indicate that in addition to having the new, favorable disposition toward God, Church saints also have the indwelling Holy Spirit. First, Jesus promised that in the future the Holy Spirit would send forth great blessings *from within* His believers (Jn. 7:38). John indicated that the Holy Spirit did not come to do this until after Jesus was glorified through His death, resurrection, and ascension (Jn. 7:39). In other words, the Holy Spirit came to do this to believers during the time of the Church.

Second, Jesus drew a distinction between the relationships of the Holy Spirit to believers before the Church and during the Church (Jn. 14:17). He indicated that before the Church the Holy Spirit dwelled *with* believers, but He promised that during the Church the Holy Spirit would be *in* believers.

Third, in Romans 8:9, 11 Paul talked about the Spirit's dwelling *in* Church saints. Fourth, in 1 Corinthians 6:19 Paul declared that the Church saint's body is a temple of the Holy Spirit and that the Spirit is *in* him. Fifth, Paul prayed that God would grant Church saints to be strengthened with power internally by His Spirit (Eph. 3:16).

The New Testament, then, indicates that Church saints possess both factors which together constitute the manner in which God administers His moral absolutes through grace. They possess the new, favorable disposition toward God (the law of God in the heart), which gives them a deep-seated moral sympathy with God's will and prompts them to will to do what God desires. They also possess the indwelling Holy Spirit, who gives them the power to do God's will. Through these two factors of His grace administration God enables Christians to live a godly life without being under the Mosaic Law administration of His moral absolutes.

EIGHTEEN

CONCLUSION

D oes a commitment to either the Covenant or Dispensational Theology position *really* make a difference? It does *not* make a difference relative to the issue of whether or not a person is a Christian. There are genuine Christians who are committed to the Covenant Theology position, and there are genuine Christians who advocate the Dispensational Theology view.

A commitment to either of these theological positions *does* make a difference, however, relative to several other issues, some of which are quite significant. That fact has been demonstrated by this book. It has been seen that Covenant and Dispensational Theology disagree concerning such matters as how God fulfills His ultimate purpose for history, how prophetic passages of the Scriptures are to be interpreted, the nature and significance of some of the biblical covenants, God's program for the nation Israel, the nature of the Kingdom of God, the beginning, nature, and distinctiveness of the Church, and the means through which the Christian is to live a godly life in this present world.

The disagreements of these two doctrinal systems relative to several of these issues have a significance which goes beyond the realm of theological theory. Some have very practical ramifications. For example, one's view concerning

God's program for Israel will affect one's attitude toward the present nation of Israel and its right to exist as an independent state in the land which it now occupies. In addition, one's view regarding the means through which the Christian is to live a godly life will affect how one approaches the matter of practical sanctification.

Doctrine determines attitudes and practice; therefore, the system of doctrine to which a person is committed does make a difference. In light of this, it is crucial that every Christian diligently search the Scriptures to determine whether it is Covenant Theology or Dispensation Theology which is presenting the biblical view.

FOOTNOTES

All Scripture references are taken from the New Scofield Reference Bible, Authorized King James Version.

CHAPTER ONE

[1]Karl Lowith, *Meaning in History* (Chicago: The University of Chicago Press, 1949), p. 1.

[2]For one such attempt see: Renald E. Showers, *What on Earth is God Doing?* (Neptune, NJ: Loizeaux Brothers, 1973).

CHAPTER TWO

[1]Louis Berkhof, *Systematic Theology* (second revised and enlarged edition; Grand Rapids: Wm. B. Eerdmans Publishing Company, 1941), P. 211.

[2]*Ibid.*

[3]Charles Caldwell Ryrie. *Dispensationalism Today* (Chicago: Moody Press, 1965), p. 179.

[4]James Orr, *The Progress of Dogma* (Grand Rapids: Wm. B. Eerdmans Publishing Co., n.d.), p. 303.

[5]Ryrie, *Dispensationalism Today*, p. 182.

[6]William G. T. Shedd, *Dogmatic Theology*, II (Grand Rapids: Zondervan Publishing House, n.d.), p. 360.

[7]Berkhof, *Systematic Theology*, pp. 269-71.

[8]*Ibid.*, p. 269.

[9]*Ibid.*, p. 270.

[10]*Ibid.*

[11]*Ibid.*, p. 215.

[12]*Ibid.*, p. 216.

[13]*Ibid.*

[14]*Ibid.*, p. 217.

[15]*Ibid.*, p. 277.

[16]*Ibid.*, p. 273.

[17]*Ibid.*

[18]*Ibid.*, p. 276.

[19]*Ibid.*, p. 286.

[20]*Ibid.*, pp. 286-87.

[21]*Ibid.*, p. 289.

[22] *Ibid.*

[23]*Ibid.*, p. 288.

[24]*Ibid.*, p. 289.

[25]*Ibid.*

[26]*Ibid.*

[27]*Ibid.*

[28]*Ibid.*, p. 288.

[29]*Ibid.*, p. 289.

[30]*Ibid.*, p. 288.

[31]Louis Berkhof, *Systematic Theology* (second revised and enlarged edition; Grand Rapids: Wm. B. Eerdmans Publishing Company, 1941), p. 293.

[32]*Ibid.*, p. 295.

[33]*Ibid.*, p. 296.

[34]*Ibid.*, p. 277.

[35]*Ibid.*

[36]*Ibid.*, pp. 282-83.

[37]*Ibid.*, p. 292.

[38]*Ibid.*, p. 293.

[39]Ernest Frederick Kevan, "Dispensation," in *Baker's Dictionary of Theology*, editor-in-chief, Everett F. Harrison (Grand Rapids; Baker Book House, 1960), p. 168.

[40]*Ibid.*

[41]*Ibid.*

[42]Louis Berkhof, *Systematic Theology*, p. 278.

[43]*Ibid.*, p. 292.

[44]*Ibid.*, p. 297.

[45]*Ibid.*, p. 299

[46]George N. M. Collins, "Covenant Theology," in *Baker's Dictionary of Theology*, editor-in-chief, Everett F. Harrison (Grand Rapids: Baker Book House, 1960), p. 144.

[47]Louis Berkhof, *Systematic Theology*, p. 279.

[48]*Ibid.*

[49]*Ibid.*

[50]*Ibid.*, p. 280.

[51]*Ibid.*, p. 277.

CHAPTER THREE

[1]Louis Berkhof, *Systematic Theology* (second revised and enlarged edition; Grand Rapids: Wm. B. Eerdmans Publishing Company, 1941), p. 298.

[2]*Ibid.*, p. 300.

[3]Bernhard W. Anderson, "The New Covenant And The Old," in *The Old Testament And Christian Faith*, ed. by Bernhard W. Anderson (New York: Herder And Herder, 1969), p. 232.

[4]Johannes Behm, "kainos," *Theological Dictionary Of The New Testament*, Vol. III, ed. by Gerhard Kittel, trans. and ed. by Geoffrey W. Bromiley (Grand Rapids: Wm. B. Eerdmans Publishing Company, 1965), p. 447.

[5]*Ibid.*

[6]*Ibid.*, p. 448.

[7]*Ibid.*, p. 449.

CHAPTER FOUR

[1]For an excellent demonstration of this, see the two-part series "Rudiments of Dispensationalism in the Ante-Nicene Period" by Larry V. Crutchfield in the July-September and October-December 1987 issues of *Bibliotheca Sacra*.

[2]A. C. Coxe (ed.), *The Ante-Nicene Fathers*, II, 476.

[3]Augustine, *To Marcellinus*, CXXXVIII, 5, 7.

[4]Charles C. Ryrie, *Dispensationalism Today* (Chicago: Moody Press, 1965), p. 71.

[5]*Ibid.*, p. 72.

[6]*Ibid.*, p. 73.

[7]William A. BeVier, "A Biographical Sketch of C. I. Scofield" (unpublished Master's Thesis, Southern Methodist University, Dallas, 1960), p. 25.

[8]*Ibid.*, p. 74.

[9]*Ibid.*, p. 95.

[10]*Ibid.*, pp. 90-91.

[11]Liddell and Scott, *An Intermediate Greek-English Lexicon* (Oxford: The Clarendon Press), p. 528.

[12]Otto Michel, "Oikonomia," *Theological Dictionary of the New Testament*, Vol. V., ed. by Gerhard Friedrich, trans. and ed. by Geoffrey W. Bromiley (Grand Rapids: Wm. B. Eerdmans Publishing Company, 1967), p. 151.

[13]*The Oxford English Dictionary* (Oxford University Press, 1933), III, p. 481.

[14]*Ibid.*, III, p. 35.

[15]Ryrie, *Dispensationalism Today*, pp. 37-38.

[16]*Ibid.*, pp. 38-39.

CHAPTER FIVE

[1]C. F. Keil and F. Delitzsch, *Biblical Commentary On The Old Testament*, Vol. I, trans. by James Martin (Grand Rapids: Wm. B. Eerdmans Publishing Company, 1959), p. 134.

[2]William F. Arndt and F. Wilbur Gingrich, *A Greek-English Lexicon Of The New Testament* (4th rev. ed.; Chicago: The University of Chicago Press, 1957), p. 851.

[3]*Ibid.*, p. 608.

[4]*Ibid.*, p. 27.

[5]Charles Caldwell Ryrie, *Dispensationalism Today* (Chicago: Moody Press, 1965), pp. 43-47.

CHAPTER SIX

[1]George R. Berry, "Covenant," *The International Standard Bible Encyclopedia*, ed. James Orr (Grand Rapids: Wm. B. Eerdmans Publishing Company, 1957), II, 727.

CHAPTER ELEVEN

[1]Edward Gibbon, *History of Christianity* (New York: Peter Eckler Publishing Company, 1916), pp. 141-42.

[2]J. C. I. Gieseler, *Text-Book of Ecclesiastical History*, Vol. I, trans. from the third German Edition by Francis Cunningham (Philadelphia: Carey, Lea, and Blanchard, 1836), p. 100.

[3]Henry C. Sheldon, *History of Christian Doctrine* (New York: Harper and Brothers, 1886), p. 145.

[4]Philip Schaff, *History of the Christian Church*, Vol. II (Grand Rapids: Wm. B. Eerdmans Publishing Company, 1973), p. 614.

[5]Adolph Harnack, "Millennium," *The Encyclopaedia Britannica*, Ninth Edition (New York: Charles Scribner's Sons, 1883), XVI, p. 314.

[6]*Ibid.*, XVI, p. 315.

[7]*Ibid.*

[8]*Ibid.*

[9]*Ibid.*

[10]*Ibid.*, XVI, p. 316.

[11]*Ibid.*

[12]Will Durant, *Caesar And Christ* (New York: Simon and Schuster, 1944), pp. 564-65.

[13]*Ibid.*, p. 575.

[14]*Ibid.*, p. 603.

[15]Elgin Moyer and Earle E. Cairns, *Wycliffe Biographical Dictionary of the Church* (Chicago: Moody Press, 1982), pp. 314-15.

[16]Irenaeus, *Against Heresies*, Book V, chpt. 33, section 4 in *The Ante-Nicene Fathers*, edited by Rev. Alexander Roberts and James Donaldson (Buffalo: The Christian Literature Publishing Company, 1885), I, p. 563.

[17]Moyer and Cairns, *Biographical Dictionary*, p. 135.

[18]*The Apostolic Fathers* in *The Fathers Of The Church*, edited by Ludwig Schopp, et. al., translated by Francis X. Glimm, Joseph M. F. Marique and Gerald G. Walsh (Washington, D.C.: The Catholic University of America Press, 1962), I, p. 378.

[19]*The Epistle of Barnabas* in *The Ante-Nicene Fathers*, edited by Rev. Alexander Roberts and James Donaldson (Buffalo: The Christian Literature Publishing Company, 1885), I. pp. 133, 135.

[20]*The Epistle of Barnabas*, chpt. 15, in *The Ante-Nicene Fathers*, I, p. 146.

[21]*Ibid.*

[22]Moyer and Cairns, *Biographical Dictionary*, pp. 220-21.

[23]Justin Martyr, *Dialogue With Trypho*, chpt. 80, in *The Ante-Nicene Christian Library*, edited by Rev. Alexander Roberts and James Donaldson (Edinburgh: T. & T. Clark, 1867), II, p. 200.

[24]*Ibid.*, chpt. 81, II, p. 201.

[25]Moyer and Cairns, *Biographical Dictionary*, p. 204.

[26]Irenaeus, *Against Heresies*, Book V, chpt. 33, section 3, I, pp. 562-63.

[27]*Ibid.*, p. 563.

[28]*Ibid.*, section 4, I, p. 563.

[29]*Ibid.*, chpt. 35, section 1, I, 565.

[30]*Ibid.*, p. 565.

[31]*Ibid.*, chpt. 36, section 3, I, p. 567.

[32]*Ibid.*, chpt. 35, section 2, I, p. 565.

[33]*Ibid.*, p. 566.

[34]Moyer and Cairns, *Biographical Dictionary*, p. 396.

[35]Tertullian, *Against Marcion*, Book III, chpt. 25 in *The Ante-Nicene Fathers*, edited by Rev. Alexander Roberts and James Donaldson (Buffalo: The Christian Literature Publishing Company, 1885), III, p. 342.

[36]*Ibid.*, p. 343.

[37]Moyer and Cairns, *Biographical Dictionary*, p. 233.

[38]*The Fathers Of The Church*, edited by Roy Joseph Deferrari, et. al., translated by Mary Francis McDonald (Washington,

D.C.: The Catholic University Of America Press, 1964), p. 49, xii-xiii.

[39]*Ibid.,* xvi.

[40]Moyer and Cairns, *Biographical Dictionary,* p. 233.

[41]*The Fathers Of The Church,* p. 49, xvii.

[42]Lactantius, *The Divine Institutes,* Book VII, chpt. 14 in *The Fathers Of The Church,* edited by Roy Joseph Deferrari, et. al., translated by Mary Francis McDonald (Washington, D.C.: The Catholic University Of America Press, 1964), pp. 49, 510.

[43]*Ibid.,* chpt. 15, pp. 49, 512.

[44]*Ibid.*

[45]*Ibid,* p. 513.

[46]*Ibid.,* chpt. 19, pp. 49, 521.

[47]*Ibid.,* chpt. 22, pp. 49, 527.

[48]*Ibid.,* chpt. 24, pp. 49, 530.

[49]*Ibid.*

[50]*Ibid.,* p. 531.

[51]*Ibid.*

[52]*Ibid.,* p. 533.

[53]*Ibid.,* chpt. 26, pp. 49, 535-36.

CHAPTER TWELVE

[1]Earnest R. Sandeen, "Millennialism," *The Encyclopaedia Britannica,* Fifteenth Edition (Chicago: Encyclopaedia Britannica, Inc., 1974), pp. 12, 201.

[2]Adolph Harnack, "Millennium," *The Encyclopaedia Britannica,* Ninth Edition (New York: Charles Scribner's Sons, 1883), XVI, p. 316.

[3]*Ibid.*

[4]*Ibid.*

[5]*Ibid.*

[6]*Ibid.*

[7]*Ibid.*

[8]Philip Schaff, *History of the Christian Church*, Vol II (Grand Rapids: Wm. B. Eerdmans Publishing Company, 1973), p. 787.

[9]*Ibid.*

[10]Sandeen, "Millennialism," pp. 12, 201.

[11]Harnack, "Millennium," XVI, p. 316.

[12]*Ibid.*

[13]Schaff, *History of the Christian Church*, II, p. 791.

[14]*Ibid.*, p. 792.

[15]*Ibid.*, pp. 618-19.

[16]Harnack, "Millennium," XVI, p. 316.

[17]*Ibid.*

[18]*Ibid.*

[19]*Ibid.*

[20]*Ibid.*

[21]*Ibid.*

[22]*Ibid.*

[23]*Ibid.*, p. 317.

[24]*Ibid.*

[25]*Ibid.*

[26]*Ibid.*

[27]*Ibid.*

[28]*Ibid.*

[29]*Ibid.*

[30]*Ibid.*

[31]Augustine, *The City of God,* Book XX, chpt. 9, trans. by Marcus Dods (New York: Random House, Inc., 1950), p. 725.

[32]*Ibid.,* pp. 725-26.

[33]Sandeen, "Millennialism," pp. 12, 202.

[34]*Ibid.*

[35]*Ibid.*

[36]Augustine, *The City of God,* Book XX, chpt. 7, p. 719.

[37]*Ibid.,* p. 720.

[38]*Ibid.*

[39]*Ibid.,* Book XX, chpt. 8, p. 722.

[40]*Ibid.,* p. 723.

[41]*Ibid.,* Book XX, chpt. 6, p. 717.

[42]Sandeen, "Millennialism," pp. 12, 202.

[43]Harnack, "Millennium," XVI, p. 317.

[44]*Ibid.*

[45]*Ibid.,* p. 318.

[46]*Ibid.*

[47]Ernest R. Sandeen, "Millennialism," *The Encyclopaedia Britannica,* Fifteenth Edition (Chicago: Encyclopaedia Britannica, Inc., 1974), pp. 12, 202.

[48]*Ibid.*

[49]*Ibid.*

[50]*Ibid.*

[51]George N. H. Peters, *The Theocratic Kingdom,* Vol. I (Grand Rapids: Kregel Publications, 1957), p. 538.

[52]*Ibid.*

[53]Sandeen, "Millennialism," pp. 12, 202.

[54]*Ibid.*

[55]*Ibid.*

[56]John F. Walvoord, *The Millennial Kingdom* (Findlay, Ohio: Dunham Publishing Company, 1959), p. 22.

[57]*Ibid.*, p. 23.

[58]Sandeen, "Millennialism," pp. 12, 202.

[59]Walvoord, *The Millennial Kingdom*, pp. 7, 23-24, 28, 30-34.

[60]Sandeen, "Millennialism," pp. 12, 202.

[61]Walvoord, *The Millennial Kingdom*, pp. 24, 31-32.

[62]Sandeen, "Millennialism," pp. 12, 202.

[63]*Ibid.*, pp. 202-03.

[64]*Ibid.*, p. 202.

[65]*Ibid.*, p. 203.

[66]Walvoord, *The Millennial Kingdom*, p. 23.

[67]Sandeen, "Millennialism," pp. 12, 203.

[68]Walvoord, *The Millennial Kingdom*, p. 23.

[69]*Ibid.*, p. 24.

[70]Earle E. Cairns, *Christianity Through The Centuries* (Grand Rapids: Zondervan Publishing House, 1954), p. 463.

[71]Elgin Moyer and Earle E. Cairns, *Wycliffe Biographical Dictionary of the Church* (Chicago: Moody Press, 1982), p. 79.

[72]"Our Fair Lady: The Statue of Liberty," *Reader's Digest*, July, 1986, pp. 53, 193-94, 197, 203.

[73]Walvoord, *The Millennial Kingdom*, p. 18.

[74]Sandeen, "Millennialism," pp. 12, 203.

[75]Walvoord, *The Millennial Kingdom*, p. 30.

CHAPTER THIRTEEN

[1]Ernest R. Sandeen, "Millennialism," *The Encyclopaedia Britannica*, Fifteenth Edition (Chicago: Encyclopaedia Britannica, Inc., 1974), pp. 12, 203.

[2]Adolph Harnack, "Millennium," *The Encyclopaedia Britannica*, Ninth Edition (New York: Charles Scribner's Sons, 1883), XVI, p. 318.

[3]Sandeen, "Millennialism," pp. 12, 203.

[4]Timothy P. Weber, *Living In The Shadow Of The Second Coming* (Grand Rapids: Zondervan Publishing House, 1983), p. 17.

[5]*Ibid.*, p. 16

[6]*Ibid.*, p. 13.

[7]*Ibid.*, pp. 32-33.

[8]*Ibid.*, p. 33

[9]*Ibid.*

[10]*Ibid.*, p. 26.

[11]*Ibid.*, p. 28.

[12] William A. BeVier, "A Biographical Sketch of C. I. Scofield" (unpublished Master's Thesis, Southern Methodist University, Dallas, 1960), pp. 20-21.

[13]Elgin Moyer and Earle E. Cairns, *Wycliffe Biographical Dictionary of the Church* (Chicago: Moody Press, 1982), p. 60.

[14]*Ibid.*, p. 155.

[15]Wilbur M. Smith, "Preface" in Vol. I of George N. H. Peters, *The Theocratic Kingdom* (Grand Rapids: Kregel Publications, 1957).

[16]Sandeen, "Millennialism," pp. 12, 203.

[17]John F. Walvoord, *The Millennial Kingdom* (Findlay, Ohio: Dunham Publishing Company, 1959), pp. 9-10.

[18]Harold O. J. Brown, "Dreams of a Third Age," *Christianity Today*, XV, No. 21 (July 16, 1971), p. 4.

[19]*Ibid.*

[20]*Ibid.*

[21]Meredith G. Kline, "Comments on an Old-New Error," *Westminster Theological Journal*, 41 (1978), pp. 172-73.

[22]Norman L. Geisler, "A Premillennial View of Law and Government," *Bibliotheca Sacra*, 142, No. 567 (July-September, 1985), p. 253.

[23]Greg L. Bahnsen, *Theonomy in Christian Ethics* (Phillipsburg, NJ: Presbyterian and Reformed Publishing Co., 1984), pp. 83-84.

[24]David Chilton, *Paradise Restored: An Eschatology of Dominion* (Tyler, TX: Reconstruction Press, 1985), p. 12.

[25]*Ibid.*, p. 214.

[26]*Ibid.*, p. 226.

[27]R. J. Rushdoony, "Government and the Christian," *The Rutherford Institute*, 1 (July-August, 1984), p. 7.

[28]Chilton, *Paradise Restored*, p. 192.

[29]Greg L. Bahnsen, "The Prima Facie Acceptability of Postmillennialism," *Journal of Christian Reconstruction*, 3 (winter, 1976-77), p. 68.

[30]*Ibid.*

[31]R. J. Rushdoony, "Postmillennialism versus Impotent Religion," *Journal of Christian Reconstruction*, 3 (winter, 1976-77), p. 126.

[32]Robert P. Lightner, "Theonomy and Dispensationalism," *Bibliotheca Sacra*, 143, No. 569 (January-March, 1986), p. 35. The author is indebted to this article for much of his information on theonomy.

[33]Baker Book House catalog, *Academic Books 1986-87,* September, 1986, p. 12.

CHAPTER FOURTEEN

[1]William F. Arndt and F. Wilbur Gingrich, *A Greek-English Lexicon of The New Testament* (4th rev. ed.; Chicago: The University of Chicago Press, 1957), p. 113.

[2]For a fuller development of God's purpose for history see: Renald E. Showers, *What On Earth is God Doing?* (Neptune, NJ: Loizeaux Brothers, 1973).

CHAPTER FIFTEEN

[1]R. B. Kuiper, *The Glorious Body of Christ* (Grand Rapids: Wm. B. Eerdmans Publishing Company, n.d.), p. 22.

[2]Charles Hodge, *Systematic Theology* (Grand Rapis: Wm. B. Eerdmans Publishing Company, 1968), 3:549.

[3]Earl D. Radmacher, *What The Church Is All About* (Chicago: Moody Press, 1978), p. 201.

[4]Louis Berkhof, *Systematic Theology* (second revised and enlarged edition; Grand Rapids: Wm. B. Eerdmans Publishing Company, 1941), p. 571.

[5]Gerhard Delling, "arche," *Theological Dictionary Of The New Testament,* Vol. I, ed. by Gerhard Kittel, trans. and ed. by Geoffrey W. Bromiley (Grand Rapids: Wm. B. Eerdmans Publishing Company, 1969), p. 479.

[6]William F. Arndt and F. Wilbur Gingrich, *A Greek-English Lexicon Of The New Testament* (4th rev. ed.; Chicago: The University of Chicago Press, 1957), p. 532.

[7]Johannes Behm, "kainos," *Theological Dictionary Of The New Testament,* Vol. III, ed. by Gerhard Kittel, trans. and ed. by Geoffrey W. Bromiley (Grand Rapids: Wm. B. Eerdmans Publishing Company, 1965), p. 447.

[8]Arndt and Gingrich, *A Greek-English Lexicon Of The New Testament*, p. 655.

[9]William F. Arndt and F. Wilbur Gingrich, *A Greek-English Lexicon Of The New Testament* (4th rev. ed.; Chicago: The University of Chicago Press, 1957), p. 356.

[10]H. E. Dana and Julius R. Mantey, *A Manual Grammar Of The Greek New Testament* (New York: The MacMillan Company, 1927), p. 191.

[11]Otto Michel, "oikodomeo," *Theological Dictionary Of The New Testament*, Vol. V, ed. by Gerhard Friedrich, trans. and ed. by Geoffrey W. Bromiley (Grand Rapids: Wm. B. Eerdmans Publishing Company, 1967), p. 139.

[12]For an excellent study of the biblical doctrine of the Church see: Earl D. Radmacher, *What The Church Is All About* (Chicago: Moody Press, 1978).

CHAPTER SIXTEEN

[1]Gerhard Delling, "katargeo," *Theological Dictionary Of The New Testament*, Vol. I, ed. by Gerhard Kittel, trans. and ed. by Geoffrey W. Bromiley (Grand Rapids: Wm. B. Eerdmans Publishing Company, 1964), p. 454.

[2]J. Oliver Buswell, *Ten Reasons Why A Christian Does Not Live A Wicked Life* (Chicago: Moody Press, 1959), p. 20.

[3]F. F. Bruce, *Commentary on the Epistle to the Hebrews*, from *The New International Commentary On The New Testament*, gen. ed., F.F. Bruce (Grand Rapids: Wm. B. Eerdmans Publishing Company, 1964), p. 143, footnote 39.

[4]*Ibid.*, pp. 145-46.

CHAPTER SEVENTEEN

[1]William F. Arndt and F. Wilbur Gingrich, *A Greek-English Lexicon Of The New Testament* (4th rev. ed.; Chicago: The University of Chicago Press, 1957), p. 157.

[2]*Ibid.*, p. 73.

[3]*Ibid.*, p. 851.

[4]For a fuller explanation of Paul's teaching in Romans 6 and 7 see: Renald E. Showers, *The New Nature* (Nepture, NJ: Loizeaux Brothers, 1986).

[5]Georg Bertram, "paideuo," *Theological Dictionary Of The New Testament*, Vol. V, ed. by Gerhard Friedrich, trans. and ed. by Geoffrey W. Bromiley (Grand Rapids: Wm. B. Eerdmans Publishing Company, 1968), p. 595.

[6]Hermann Cremer, *Biblico-Theological Lexicon Of New Testament Greek*, trans. by William Urwick (4th English ed.; Edinburgh: T. & T. Clark, 1895), p. 812.

[7]Homer A. Kent, *The Pastoral Epistles* (Chicago: Moody Press, 1958), p. 234.

[8]James Comper Gray, *The Biblical Museum*, Vol. IV (New York: Anson D. F. Randolph & Company, n.d.), p. 120.

[9]Norman C. Habel, "Jeremiah, Lamentations," of *Concordia Commentary*, ed. by Walter J. Bartling and Albert E. Glock (Saint Louis: Concordia Publishing House, 1968), p. 247.

[10]W. H. Bennett, "The Book of Jeremiah," of *The Expositor's Bible*, ed. by W. Robertson Nicoll (New York: Funk & Wagnalls Company, 1900), p. 353.

[11]C. F. Keil, "The Prophecies of Jeremiah," in *Biblical Commentary on the Old Testament*, trans. by David Patrick (Grand Rapids: Wm. B. Eerdmans Publishing Company, 1949-50), II, p. 40.

[12]John Calvin, *Commentaries on the Book of the Prophet Jeremiah and the Lamentations*, trans. and ed. by John Owen (Grand Rapids: Wm. B. Eerdmans Publishing Company, 1950), IV, p. 130.

[13]H. L. Ellison, *Ezekiel: The Man and His Message* (Grand Rapids: Wm. B. Eerdmans Publishing Company, 1956), p. 128.

[14]Norman H. Snaith, *The Distinctive Ideas of the Old Testament* (New York: Schocken Books, 1964; London: Epworth Press, 1944 and 1983), p. 146.

[15]*Ibid.*, p. 154.

[16]Ellison, *Ezekiel*, p. 128.

[17]John T. Demarest, *A Commentary on the Second Epistle of the Apostle Peter (New York: Sheldon & Co., 1862), p. 89.*

[18]*For a fuller study of the Jeremiah 31, Ezekiel 36, and New Testament passages of this article see: Renald E. Showers, The New Nature* (Nepture, NJ: Loizeaux Brothers, 1986).

MORE BOOKS BY RENALD E. SHOWERS

THE MOST HIGH GOD
One of the finest commentaries on the book of Daniel available today, this clear, concise, and consistently premillennial exposition sheds tremendous light on prophecy, the Times of the Gentiles, and other portions of the prophetic Word.
ISBN-10: 0-915540-30-4, #B26
ISBN-13: 978-0-915540-30-3

MARANATHA: OUR LORD, COME!
A Definitive Study of the Rapture of the Church
This in-depth study addresses such issues as the Day of the Lord, its relationship to the Time of Jacob's Trouble and the Great Tribulation, the 70 Weeks of Daniel, and much more. Learn why the timing of the Rapture has practical implications for daily living and ministry.
ISBN-10: 0-915540-22-3, #B55P
ISBN-13: 978-0-915540-22-8

THOSE INVISIBLE SPIRITS CALLED ANGELS
Much is being said about angels these days. How much of it is correct? This excellent, easy-to-read volume teaches what the Bible says about angels—who they are, what they do, and how they minister to us.
ISBN-10: 0-915540-24-X, #B66
ISBN-13: 978-0-915540-24-2

Two Millennia of Church History

This comprehensive, easy-to-understand, and beautifully illustrated 24-page booklet puts 2,000 years of church history at your fingertips. An exceptional resource, it will enable you to trace the development of first-century Orthodoxy, Romanism, the Reformation, liberal theology, the great spiritual awakenings, and much, much more.

ISBN-10: 0-915540-67-3, #B82
ISBN-13: 978-0-915540-67-9

The Foundations of Faith

Volume 1

This is a compiliation of Dr. Showers' in-depth studies in systematic theology. *The Revealed and Personal Word of God* is the first in the series and covers bibliology and Chrisology—the doctrines of the Bible and the Messiah. This hardback, fully indexed volume is a must for any serious student of God's Word.

ISBN-10: 0-915540-77-0, #B89
ISBN-13: 978-0-915540-77-8

What on Earth Is God Doing?

Satan's Conflict With God—Updated and Revised
Walk from creation to eternity in a compact, exciting, easy-to-read format guaranteed to change the way you look at the world. This revised edition is packed with new material to help you understand the war Satan is waging against God and how that conflict affects history, the persecution of Jewish people and Christians, and the direction the world is heading.

ISBN-10: 0-915540-80-0, #B44
ISBN-13: 978-0-915540-80-8